St. Jacobs, St. Clements Ontario and Area in Colour Photos, Saving Our History One Photo at a Time

Photography
by Barbara Raué
2014

Series Name:
Cruising Ontario

Book 72: St. Jacobs, St. Clements
and Area

Cover photo: 20 Isabella Street, St. Jacobs

Series Name: Cruising Ontario
Saving Our History One Photo at a Time

Other Books by Barbara Raue

Coins of Gold

Arrows, Indians and Love

The Life and Times of Barbara
Volume 1: Inventions That Have Enhanced My Life
Volume 2: Entertainment That I Have Enjoyed
Volume 3: East Coast Trips
Volume 4: Olympics Have Always Intrigued Me
Volume 5: Wonders of the World
Volume 6: Caribbean Cruises We Have Enjoyed
Volume 7: Animals
Volume 8: Storms and Other Major Disasters in My Lifetime
Volume 9: Wars, Terrorist Attacks and Major Disasters

The Cromwell Family Book

Laura Secord Discovered

Visit Barbara's website to view all of her books
http://barbararaue.ericraue.com

St. Jacobs

St. Jacobs is located in southwest Ontario just north of Waterloo. It is a popular location for tourism due to its Mennonite heritage and retail focus. The Conestogo River, which powered the village's original gristmill, runs through the village.

St. Jacobs was settled in 1819 and was first known as "Jakobstettel" which means "Jacob's Village" or "James's Village". The *St.* was added to the name simply to make it sound more pleasing and the pluralization was in honour of the combined efforts of Jacob C. Snider and his son, Jacob C. Snider, Jr., founders of the village.

St. Jacobs' developed as a thriving business community throughout the 1800s with such businesses as a felt factory, tannery, glue factory, flour mill, saw mill, and furniture factory. The village served the needs of surrounding pioneer farm settlements. Situated on Arthur Road, St. Jacobs boasted four hotels by 1852. One of these - Benjamin's Restaurant and Inn - is still operating today.

St. Jacobs features dozens of artisans in historic buildings, such as the Country Mill, Village Silos, Mill Shed, and the Old Factory. Visitors may watch artisans make pottery, quilts, designer clothes, jewellery, glass vases, woven wall hangings, tiffany lamps, stained glass doors, miniature doll houses, and more. There are also two blacksmith shops to visit. The Visitor Centre is a Mennonite interpretation centre providing information and education on the Mennonite people in the community.

St. Clements, Heidelberg, Crosshill and Bamberg are communities in the Township of Wellesley.

Table of Contents

St. Jacobs

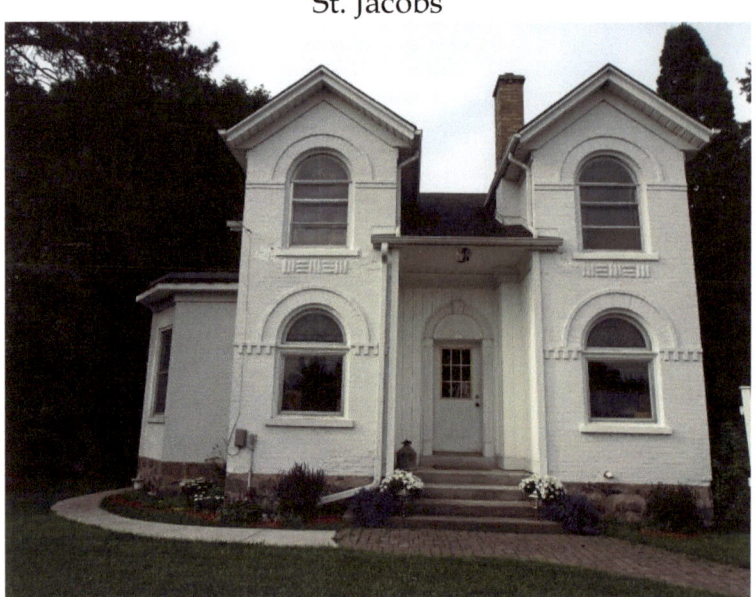

Boyhood home of Darryl Sittler, National Hockey League player for the Toronto Maple Leafs

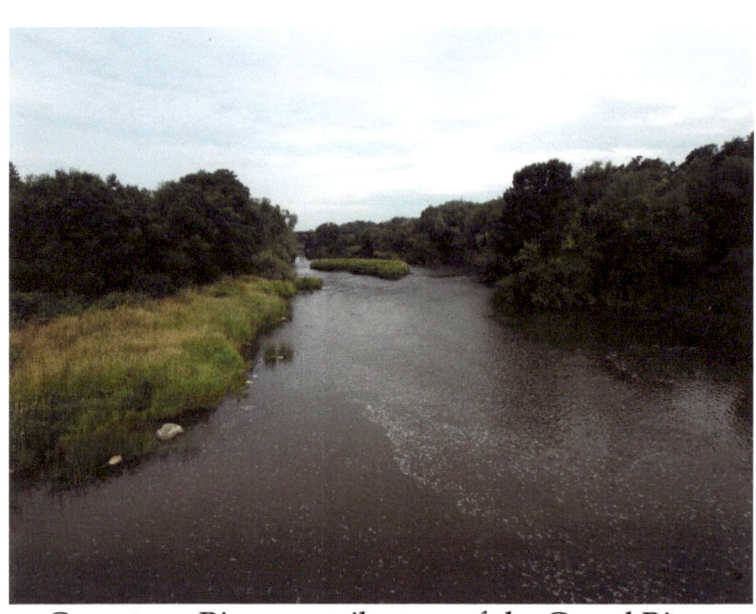

Conestogo River – a tributary of the Grand River

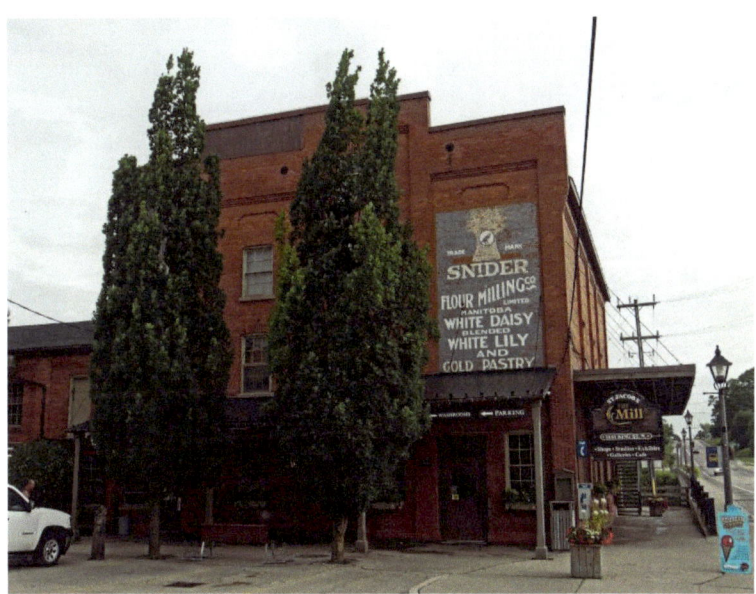

The Mill - 1441 King Street North

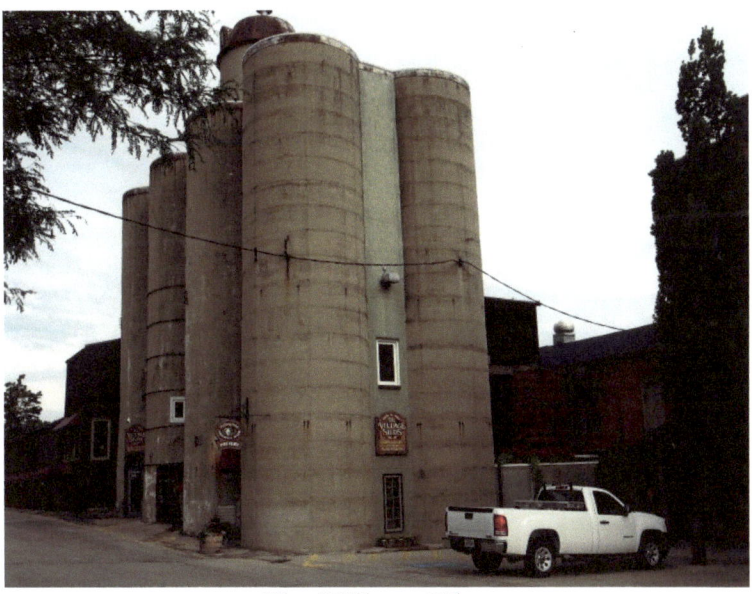

The Village Silos

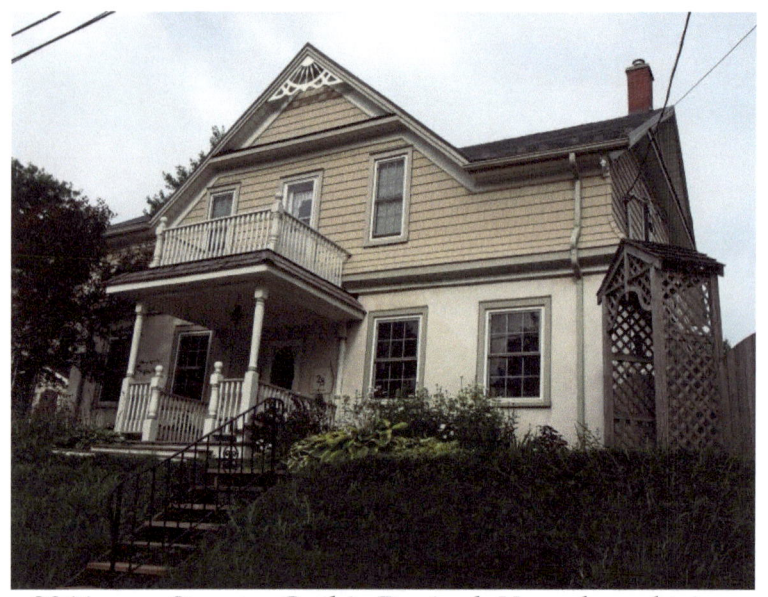

28 Young Street – Gothic Revival, Vergeboard trim, Balcony on second floor

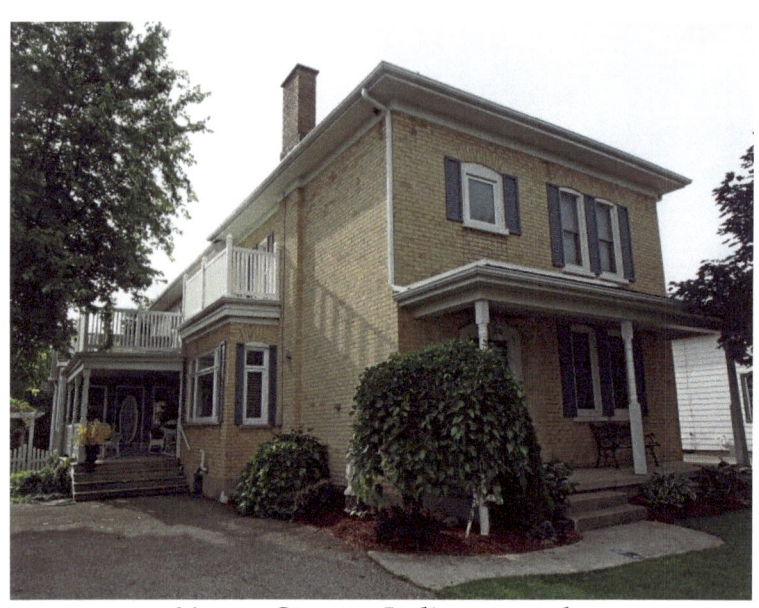

Young Street – Italianate style

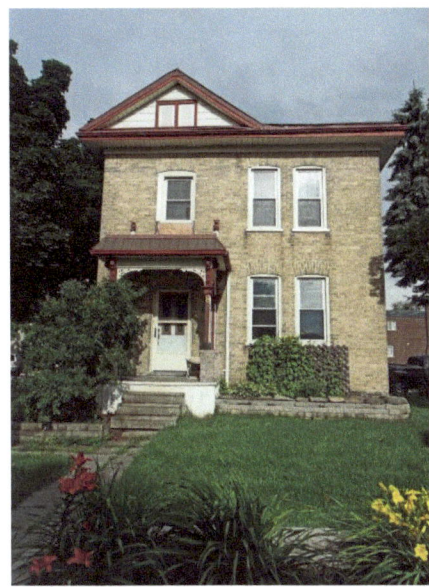
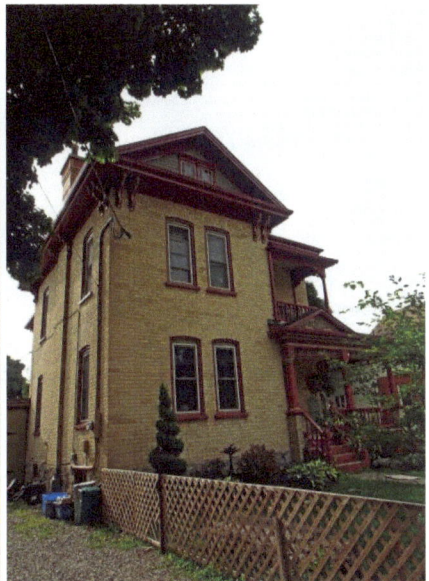

8 Young Street   23 Young Street
Italianate style
Cornice brackets

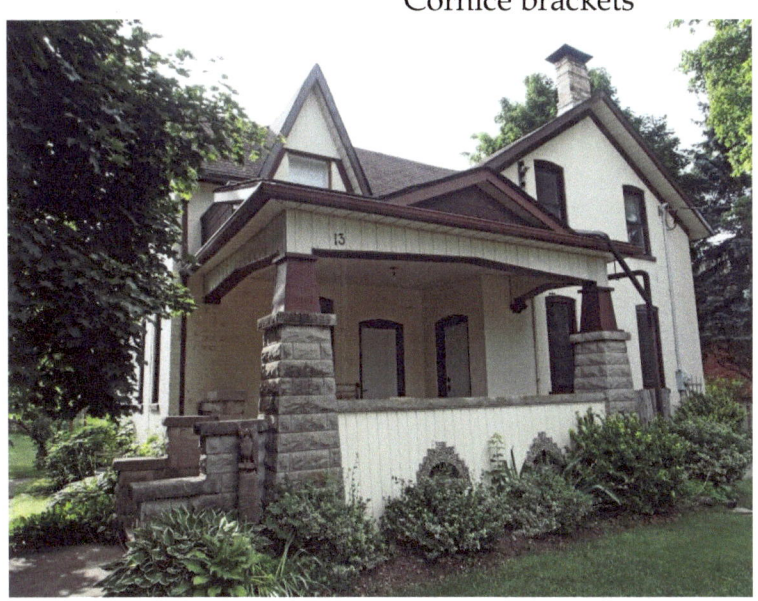

13 Young Street – Gothic Revival

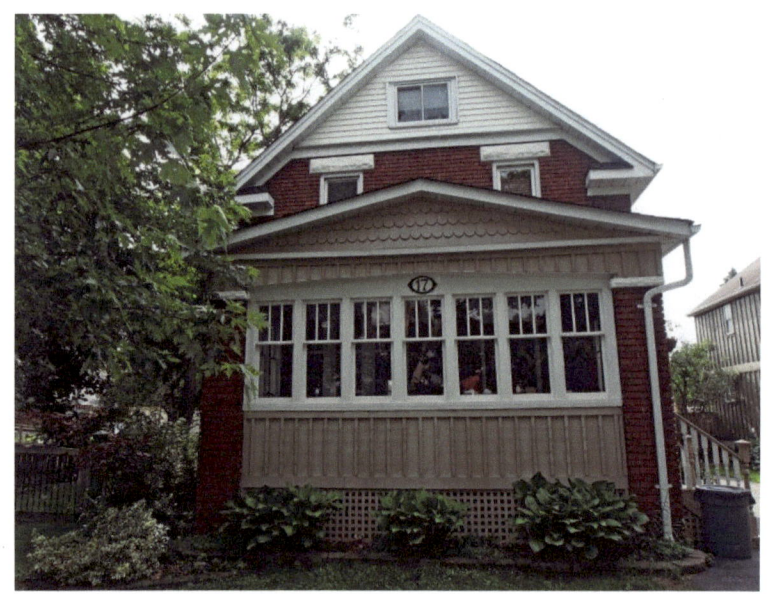

17 Young Street – Edwardian style

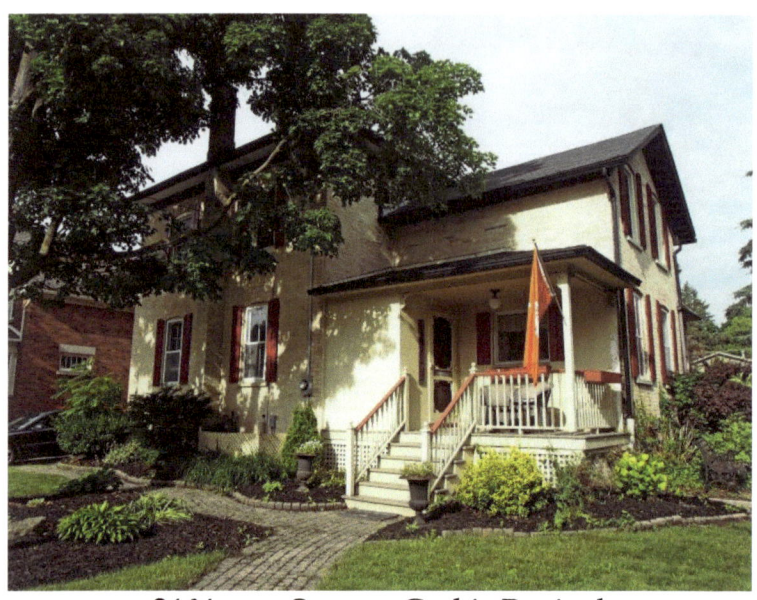

24 Young Street – Gothic Revival

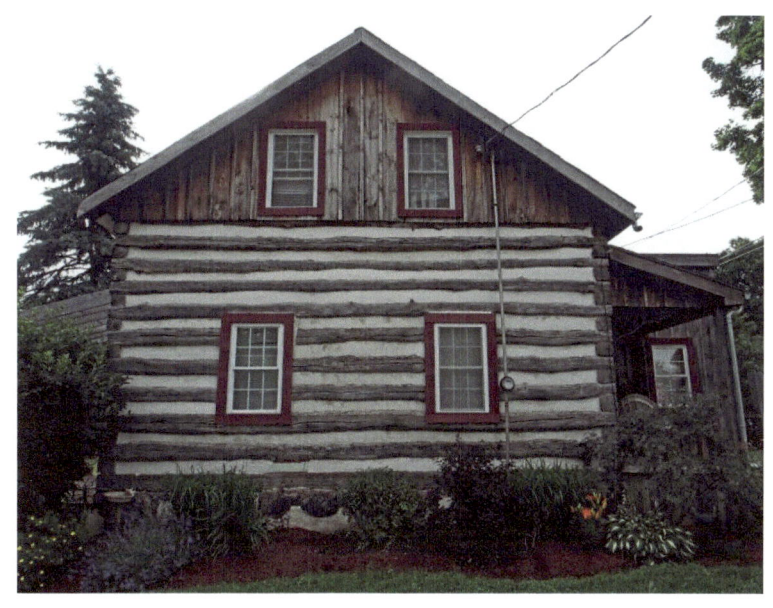

Log Cabin

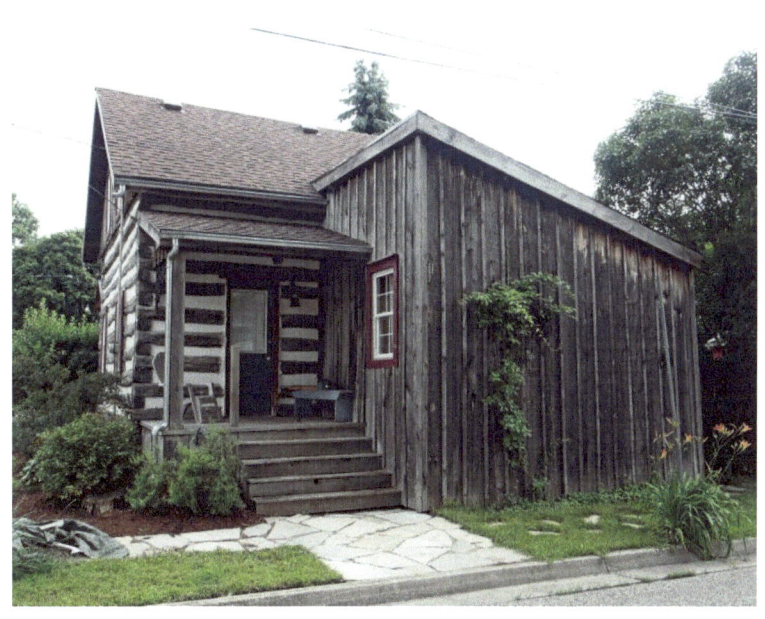

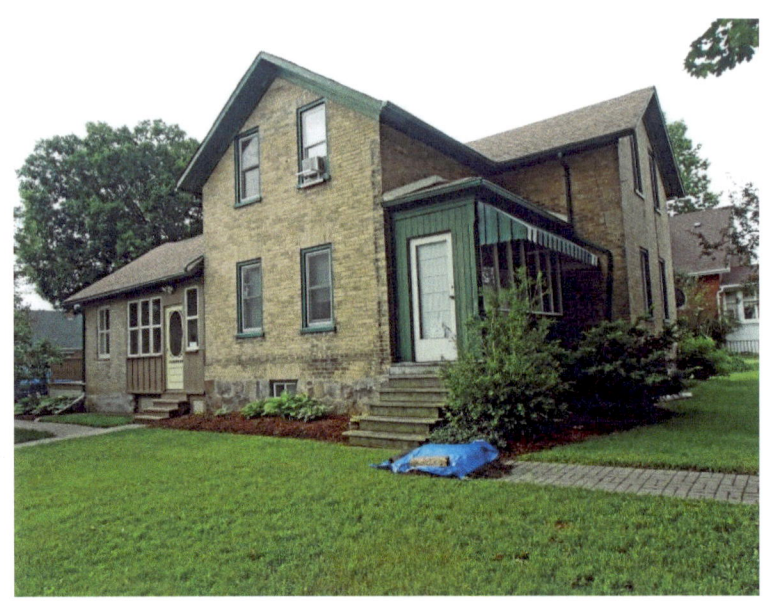

35 Young Street – Gothic Revival in yellow brick

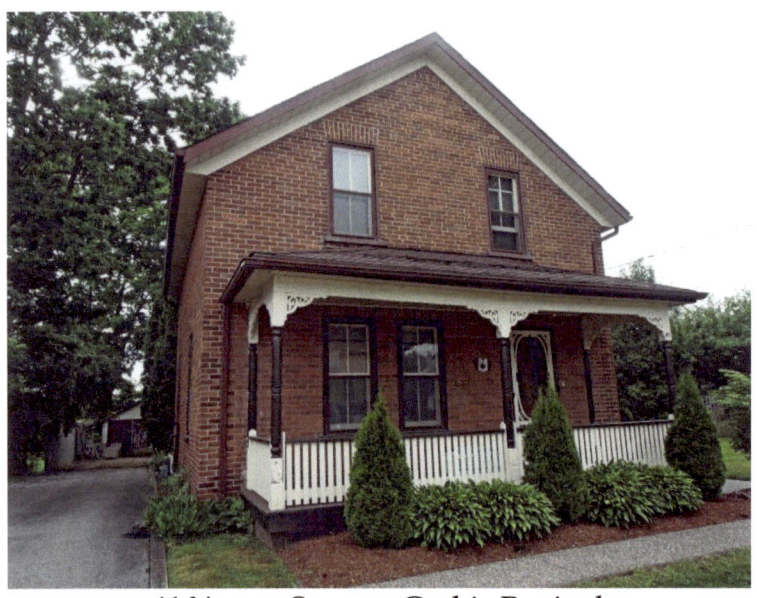

41 Young Street – Gothic Revival

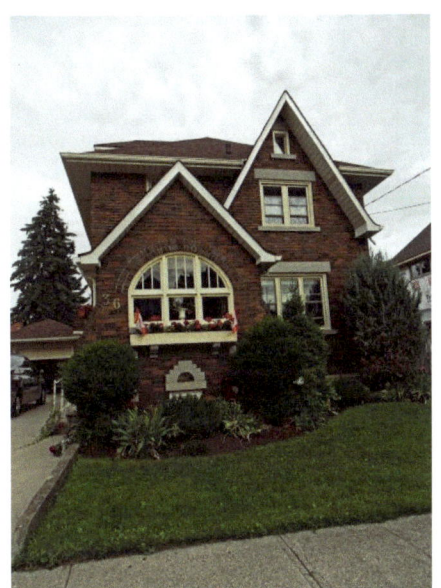

36 Young Street

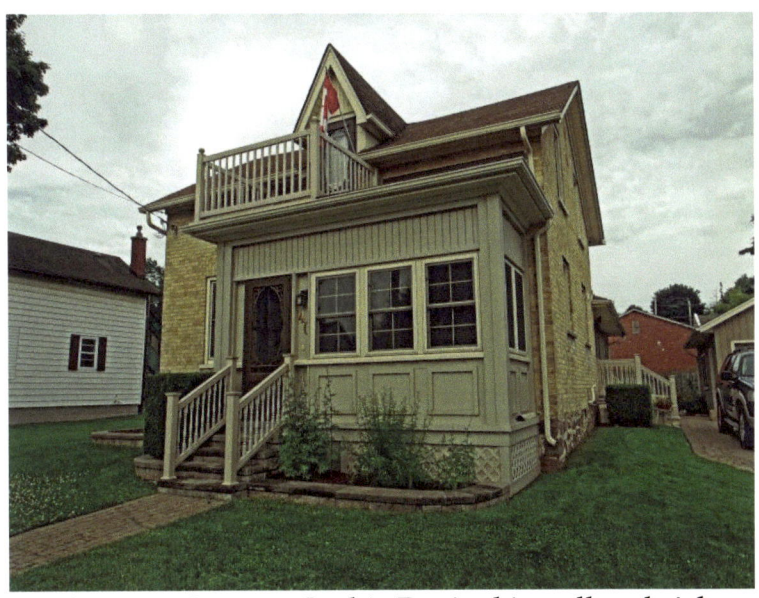

40 Young Street – Gothic Revival in yellow brick

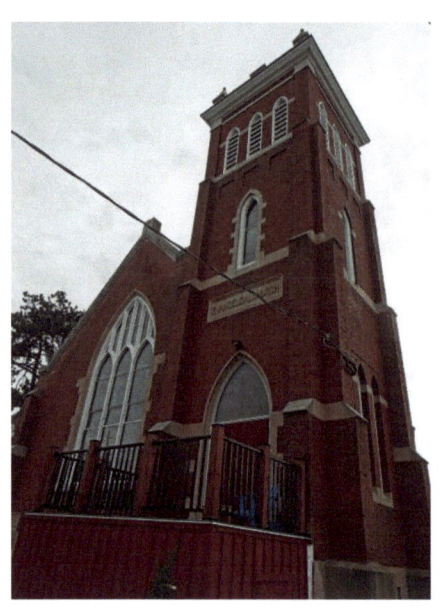

Evangelical Church – King Street c. 1914

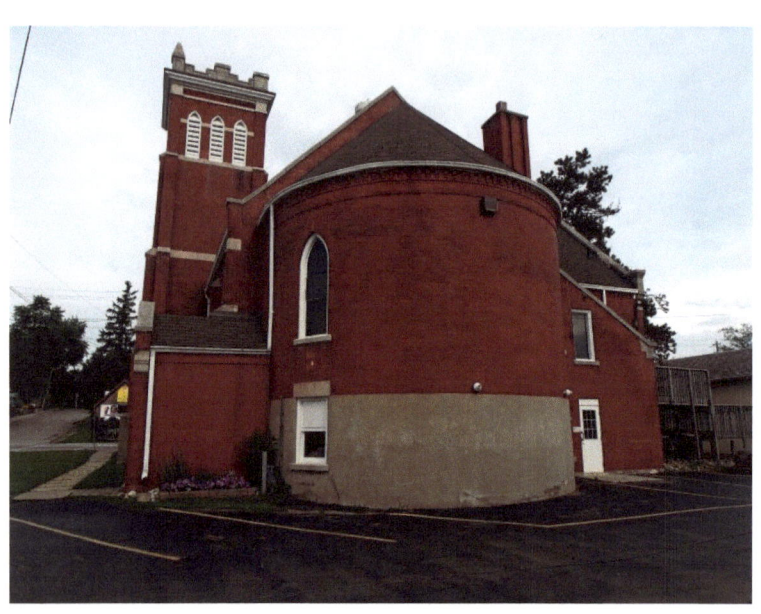

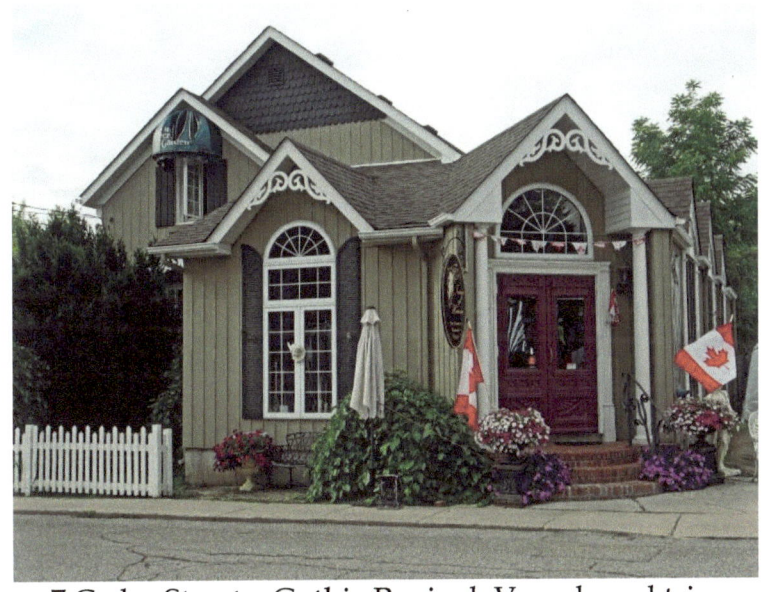

7 Cedar Street – Gothic Revival, Vergeboard trim

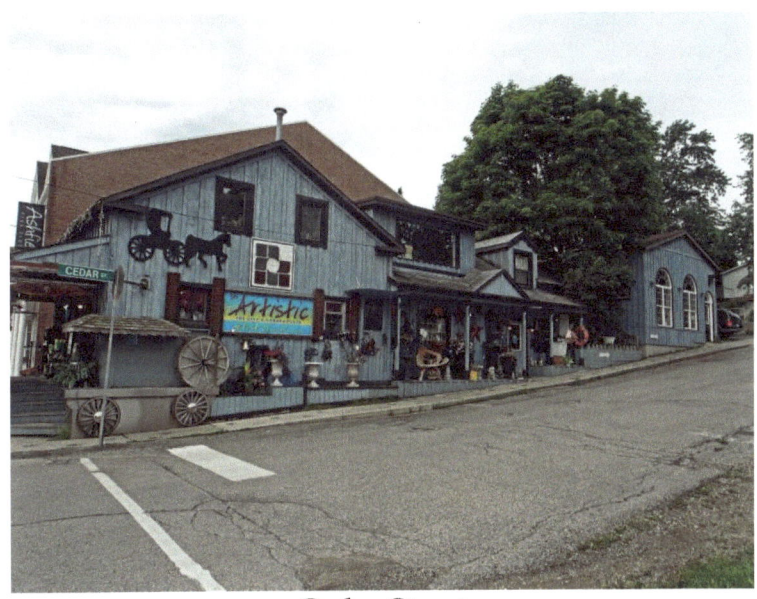

Cedar Street

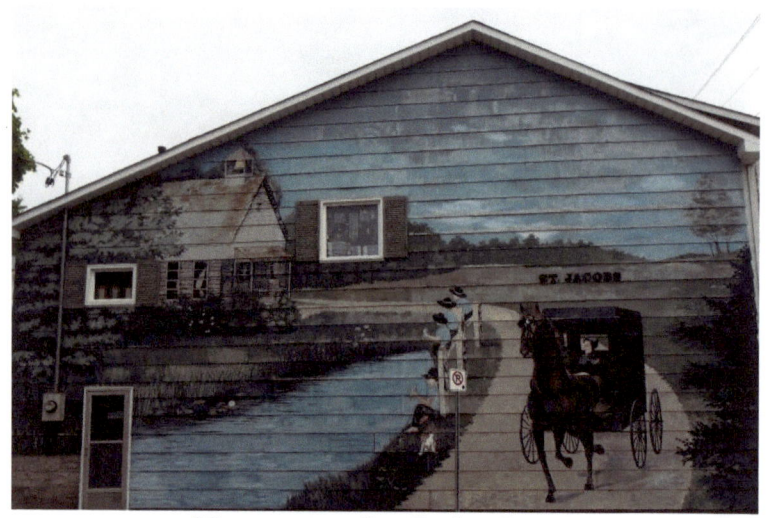

House mural – Cedar Street

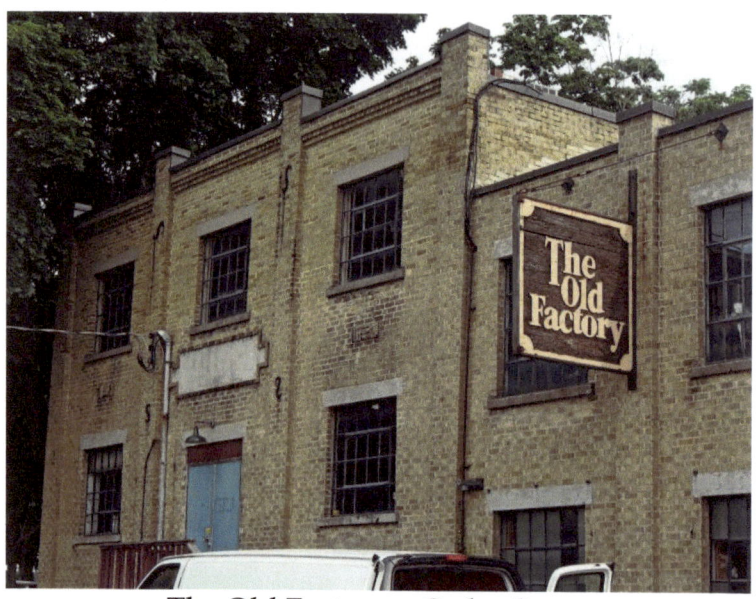

The Old Factory – Cedar Street

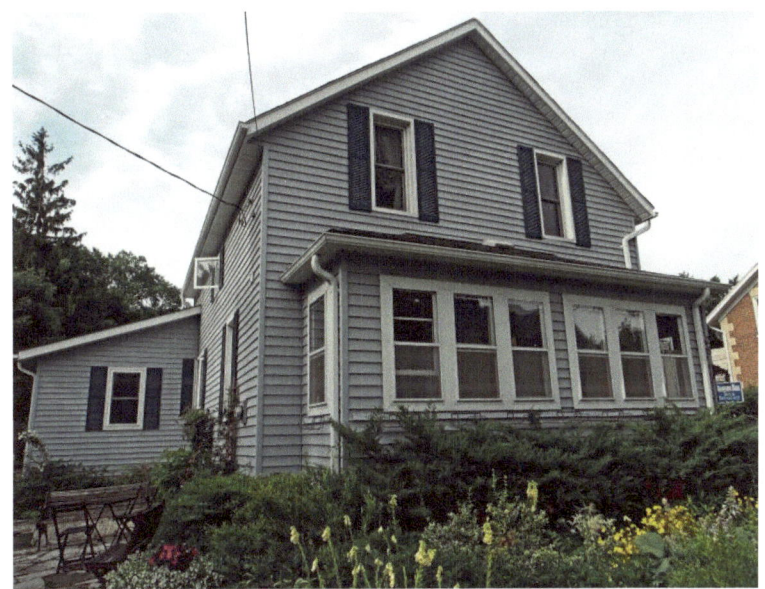

25 Spring Street – Bauman Haus Bed and Breakfast
Gothic Revival

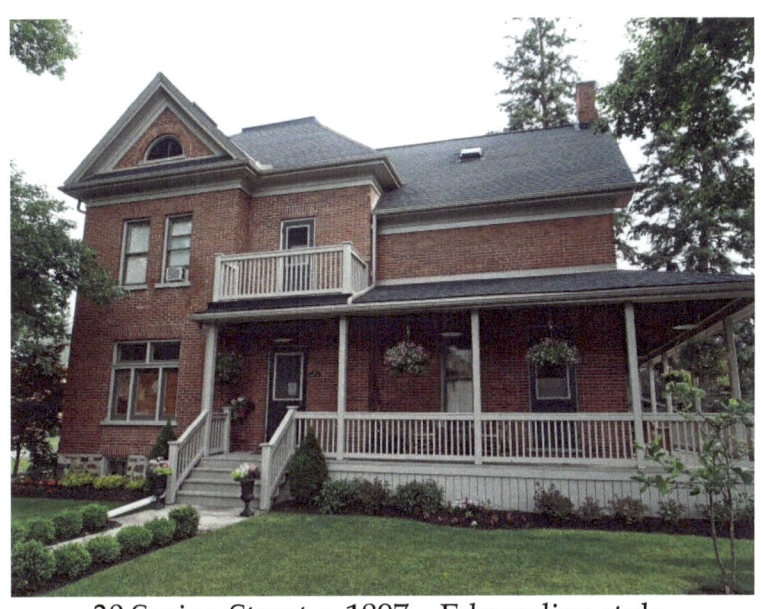

30 Spring Street c. 1897 – Edwardian style,
Balcony on second floor, wraparound verandah

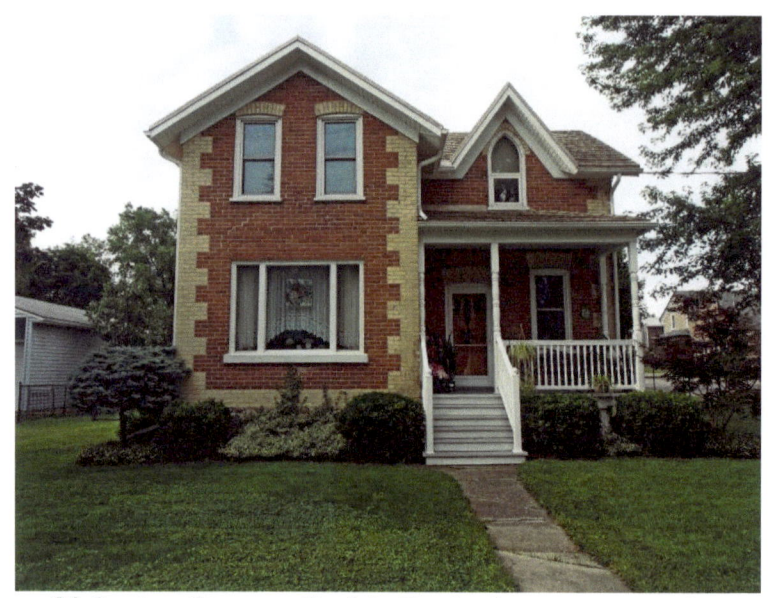

20 Spring Street – Gothic Revival – corner quoins

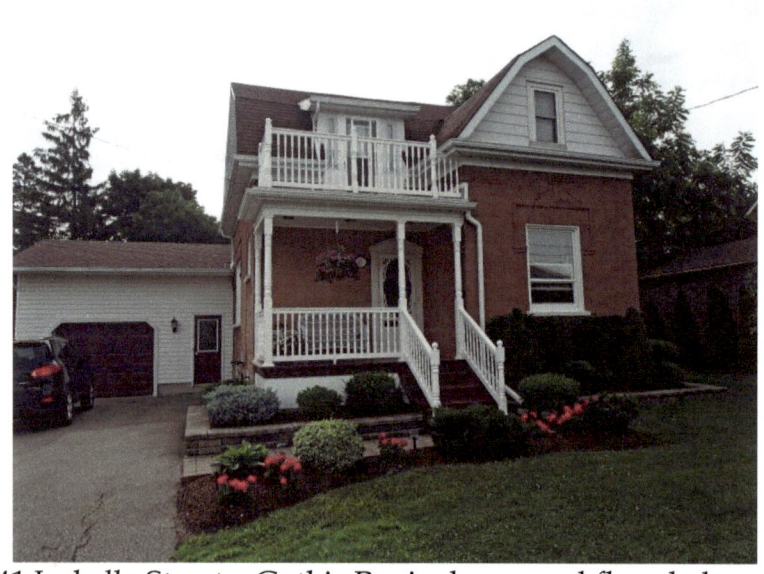

41 Isabella Street – Gothic Revival – second floor balcony

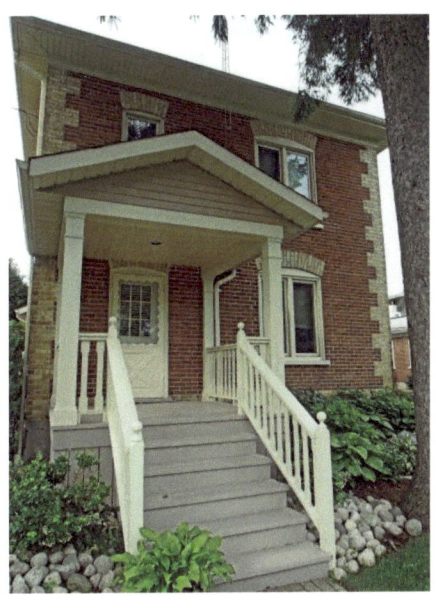

34 Isabella Street – Italianate, corner quoins

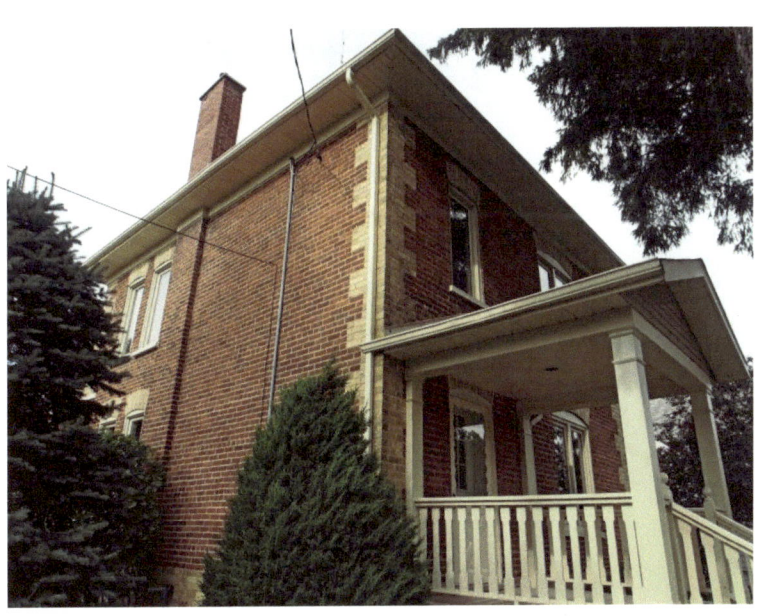

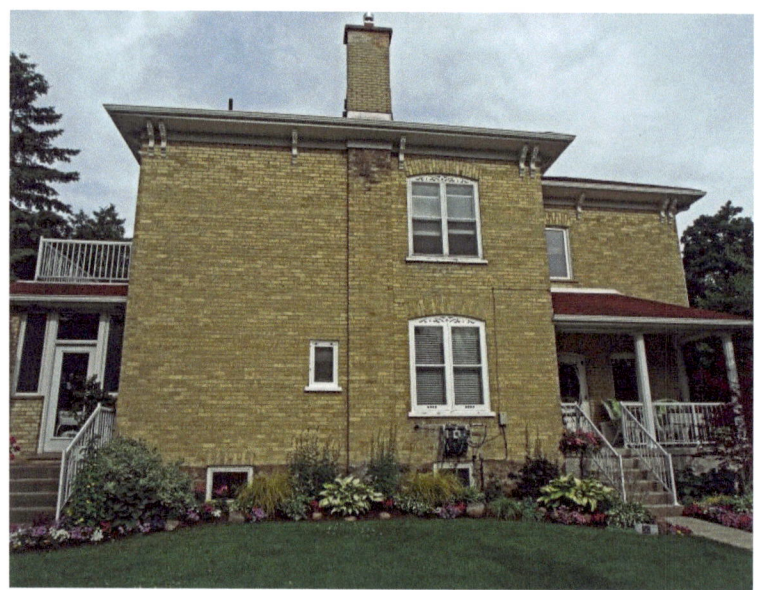

28 Isabella Street – Italianate – cornice brackets

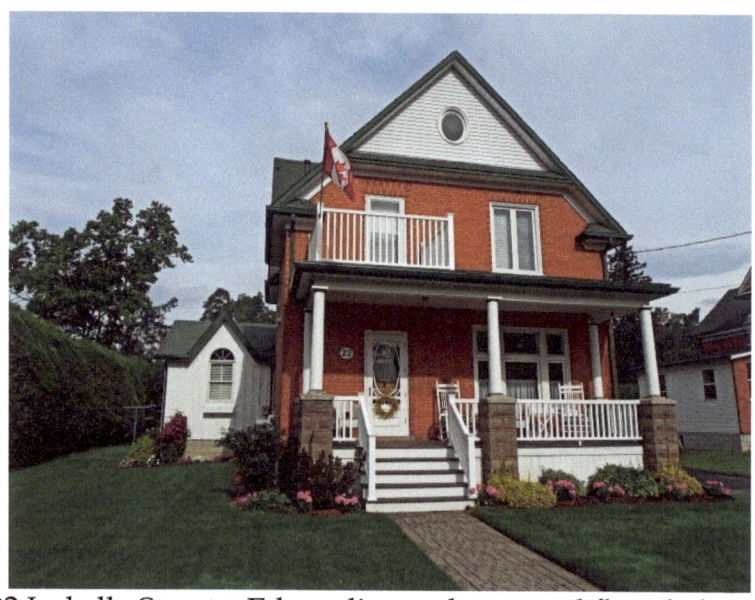

22 Isabella Street – Edwardian style, second floor balcony

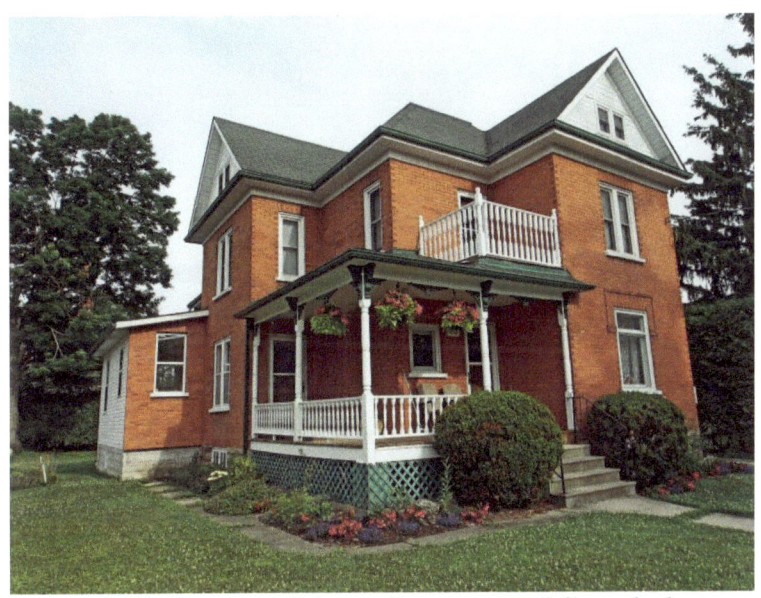

20 Isabella Street – Edwardian, second floor balcony

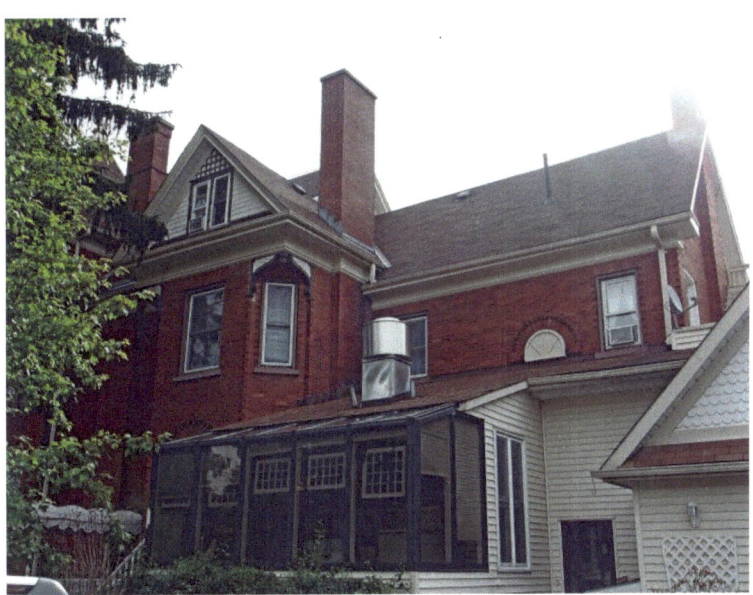

Isabella Street - Edwardian

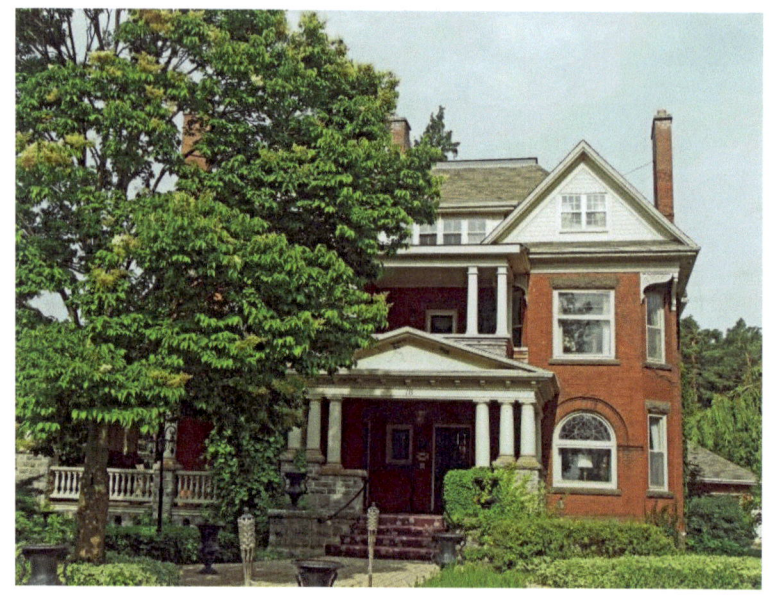

16 Albert Street – Edwardian style with Italianate features

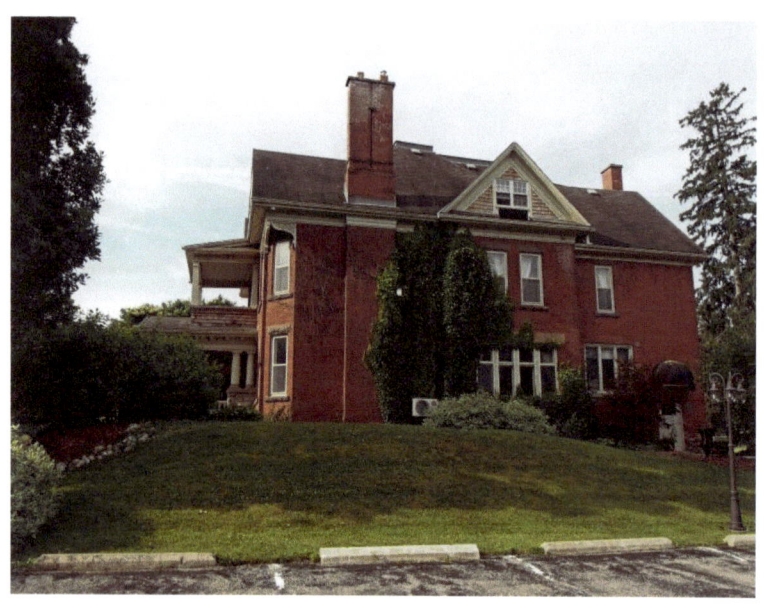

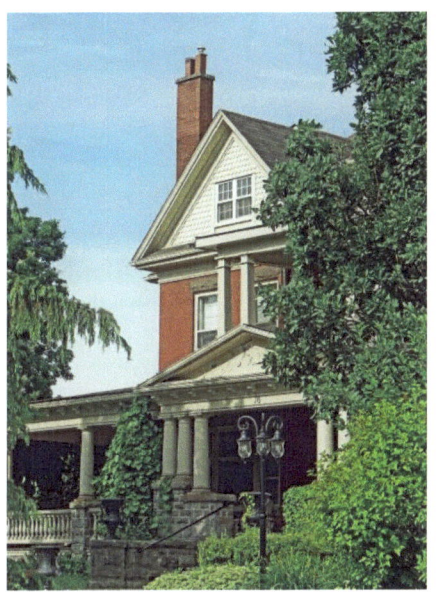

16 Albert Street

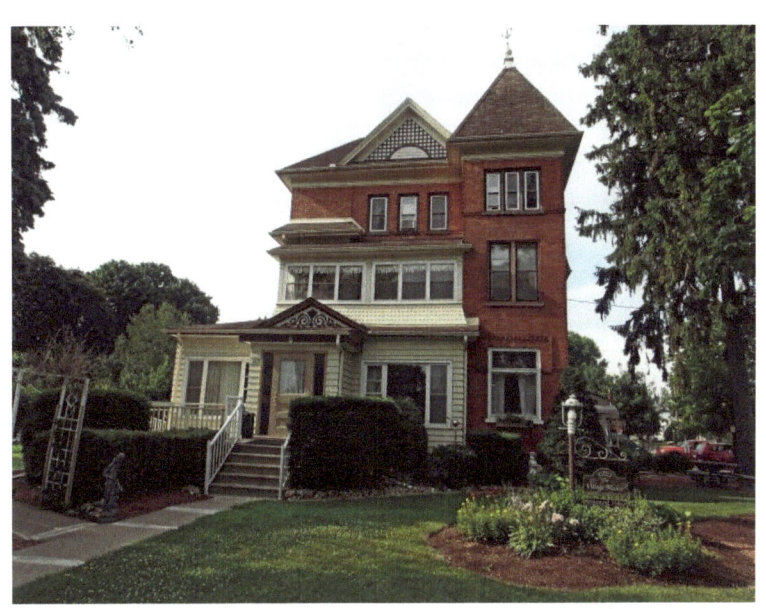

29 Albert Street – Queen Anne style

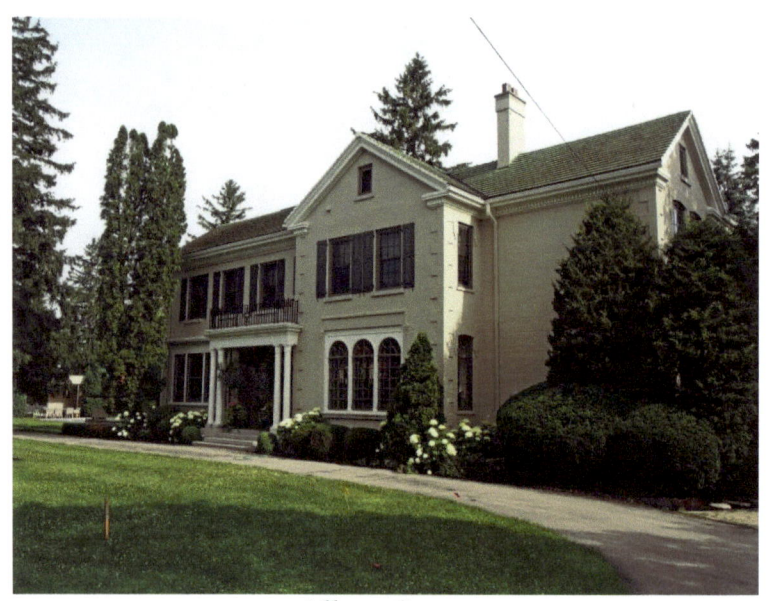

Albert Street

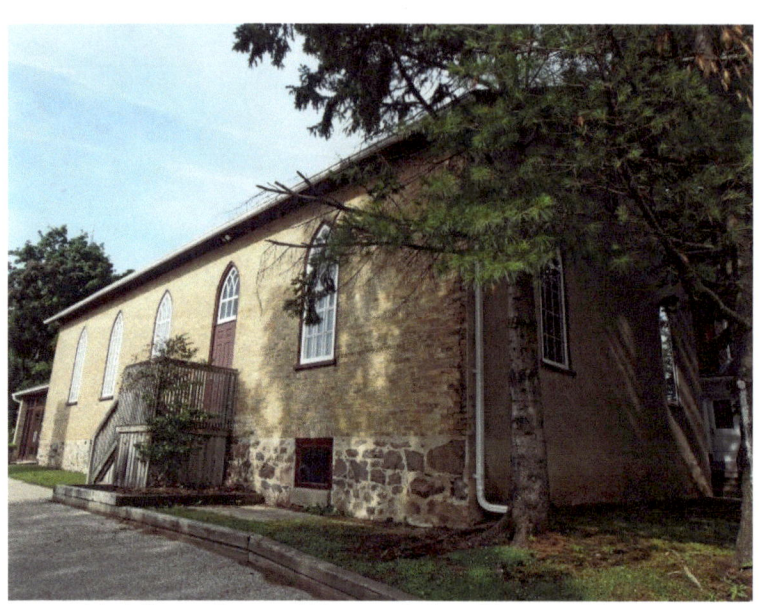

11 Albert Street West – Schoolhouse Theatre
Cobblestone basement wall

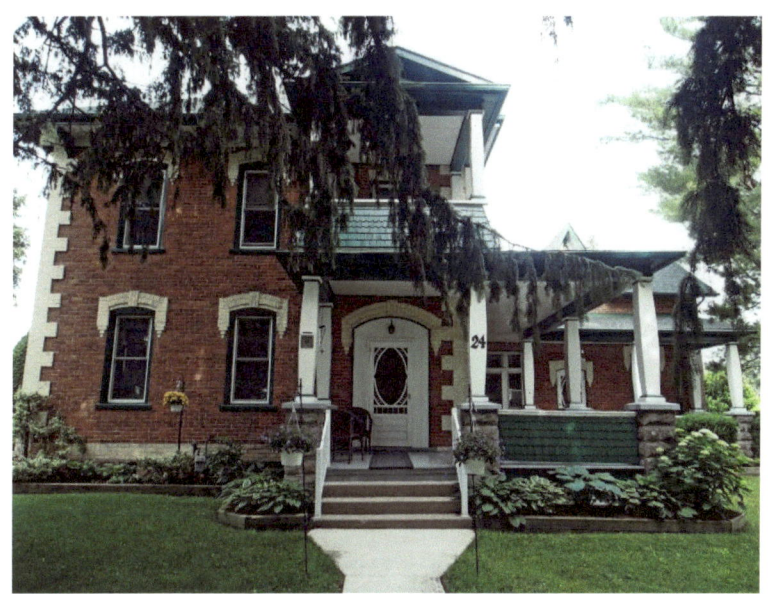

24 Queensway Drive – corner quoin

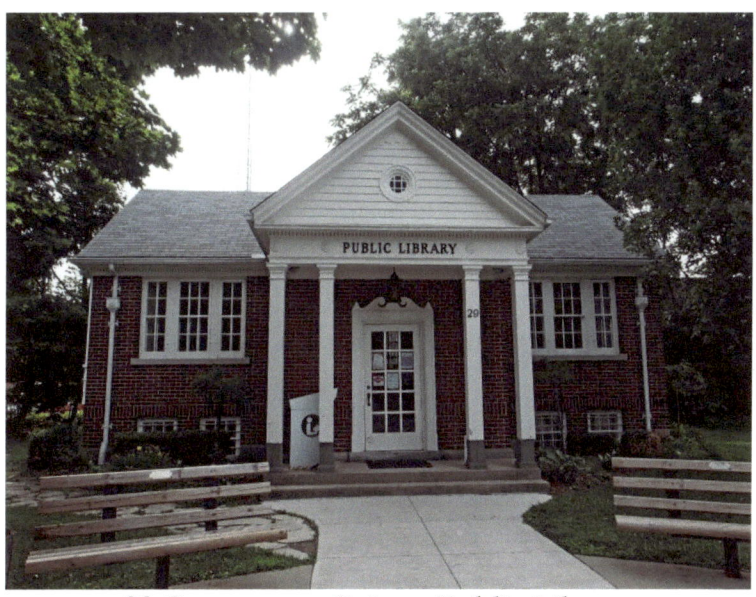

29 Queensway Drive - Public Library

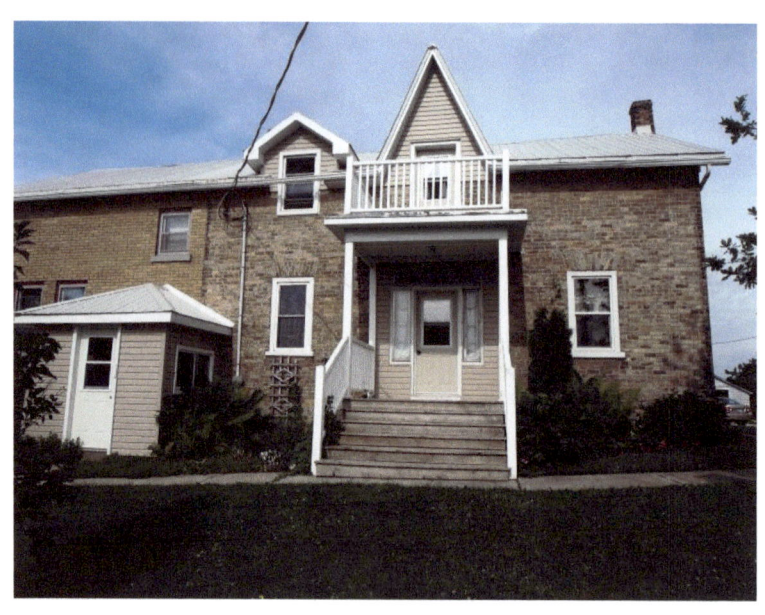

Farmhouse and Barn

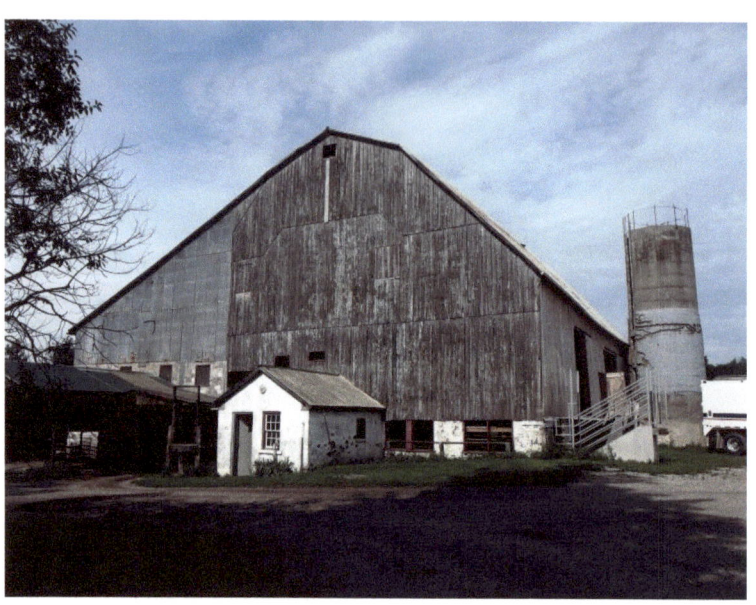

St. Clements

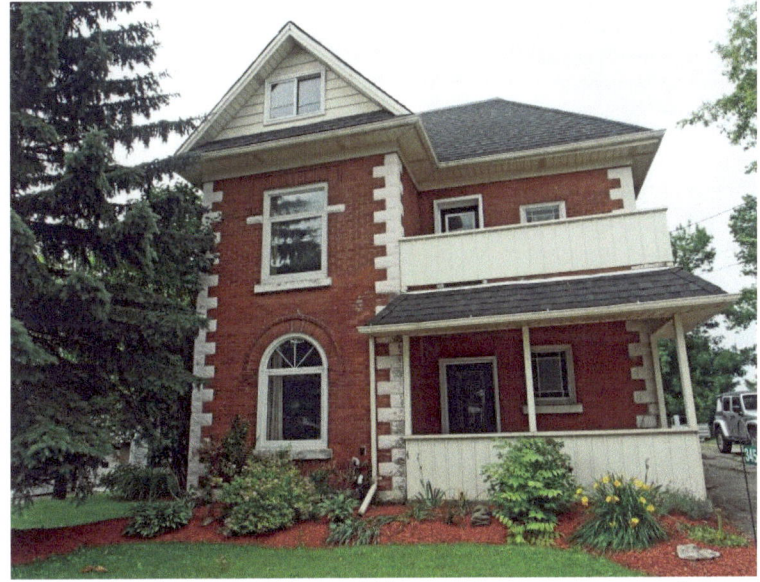

3455 Lobsinger Line – Edwardian, corner quoins

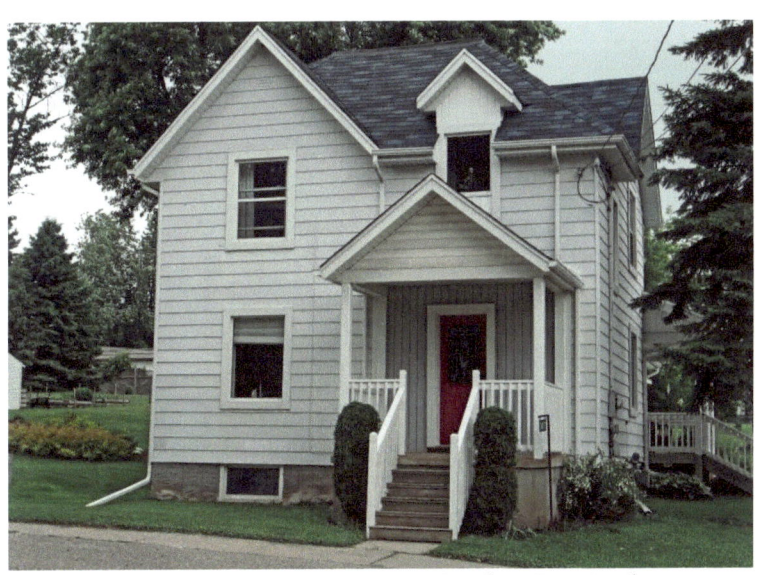

3454 Lobsinger Line – Gothic Revival

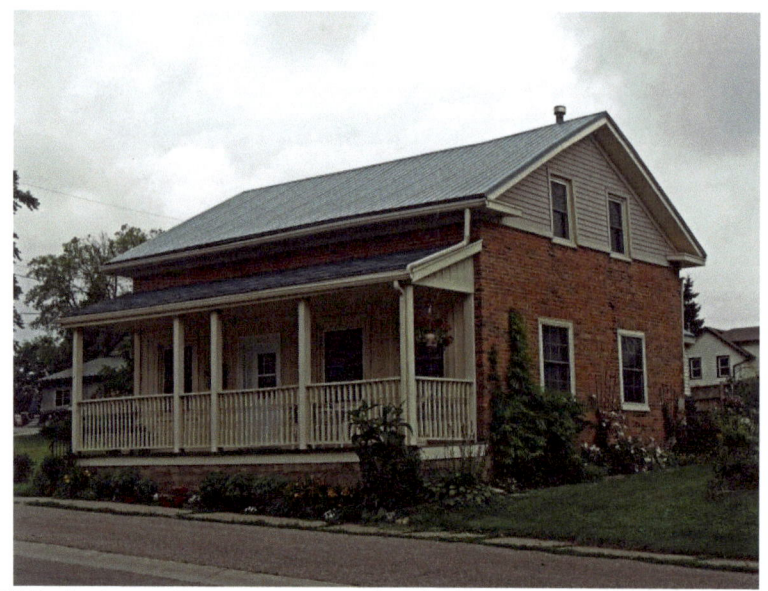

3465 Lobsinger Line – one-and-a-half storey side gable Gothic
with cornice return on gable

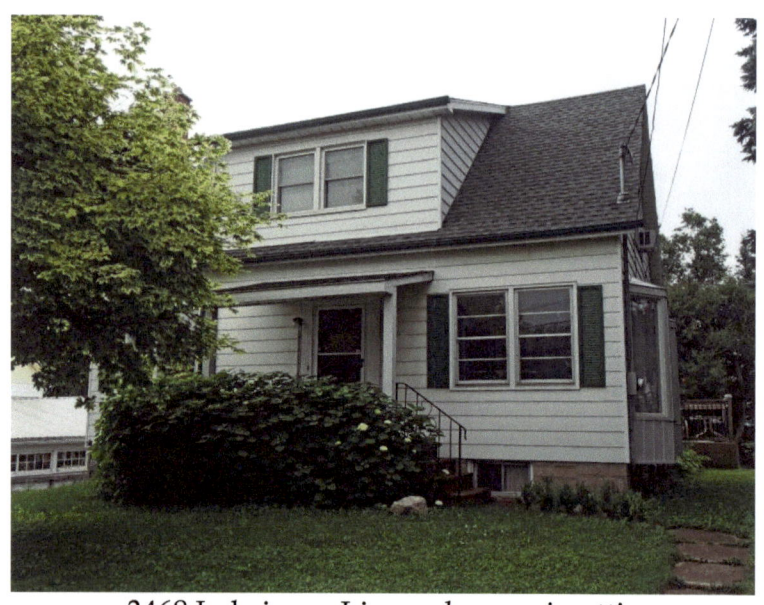

3468 Lobsinger Line – dormer in attic

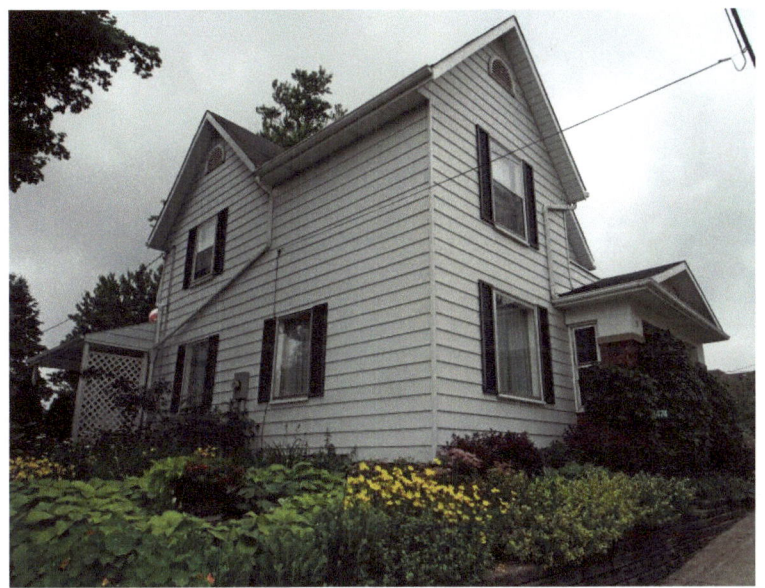

3474 Lobsinger Line – Gothic Revival

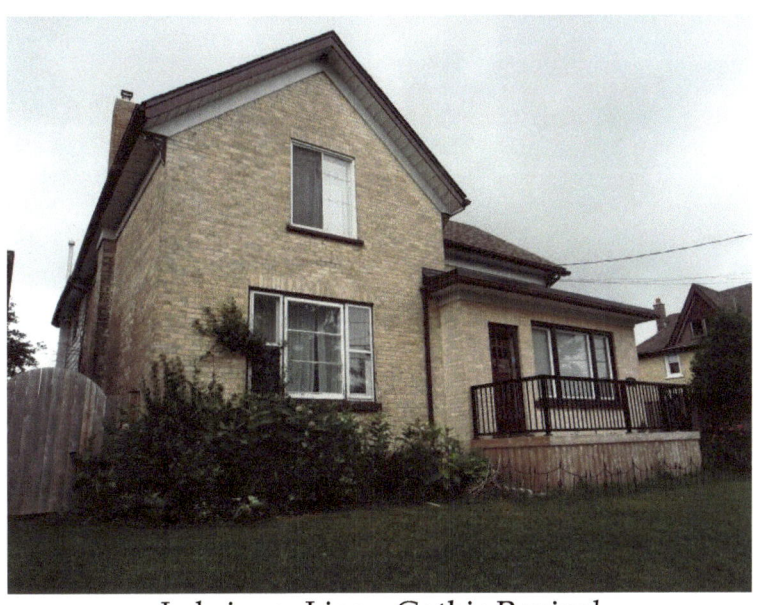

Lobsinger Line – Gothic Revival

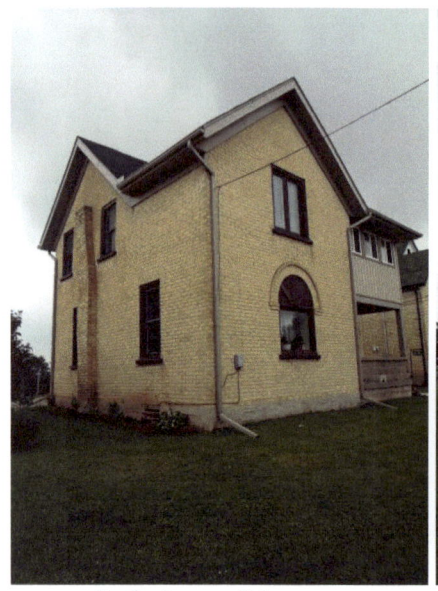 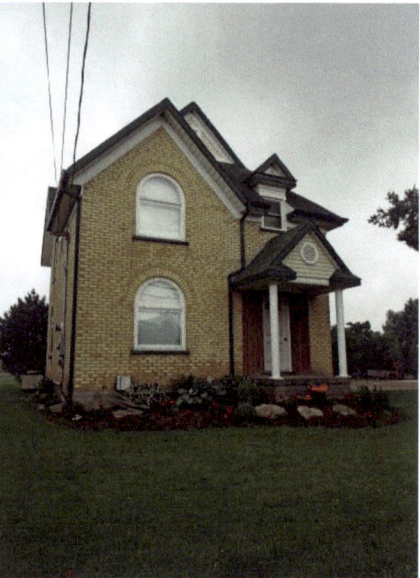

Lobsinger Line   3522 Lobsinger Line
                    Gothic Revival

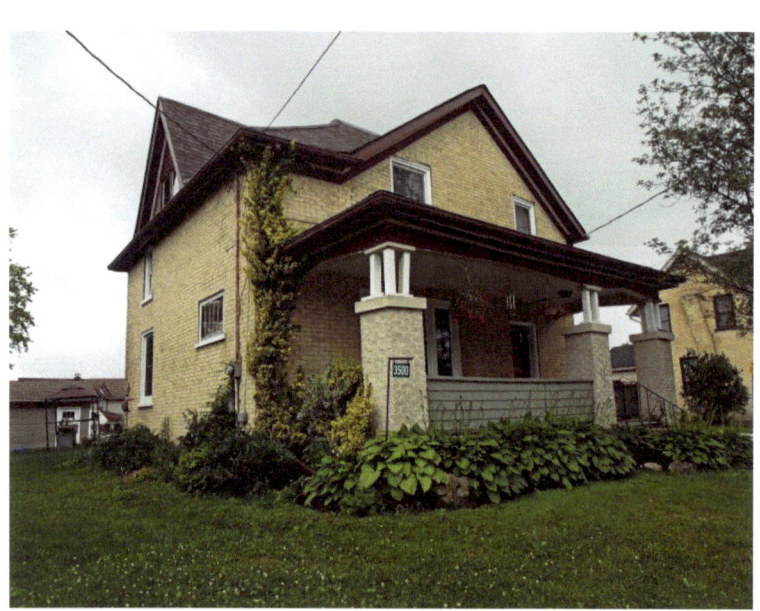

3500 Lobsinger Line – Gothic Revival

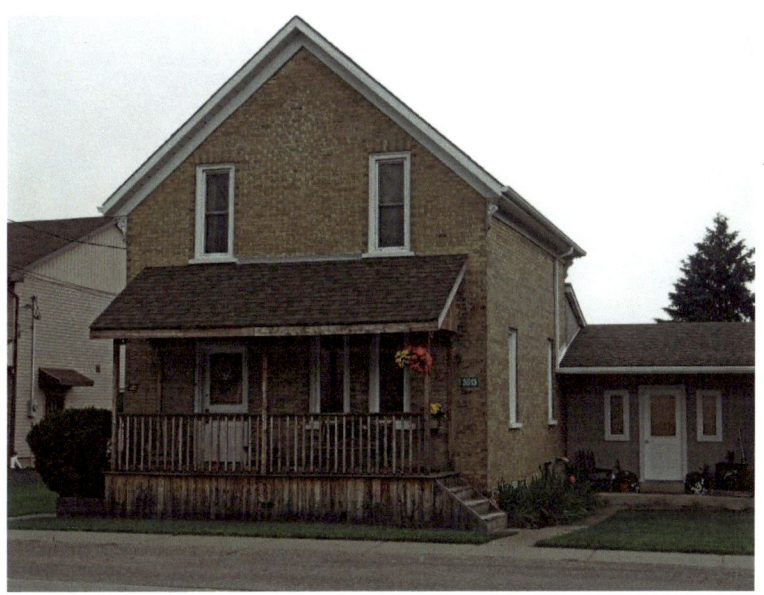

3513 Lobsinger Line – Gothic Revival

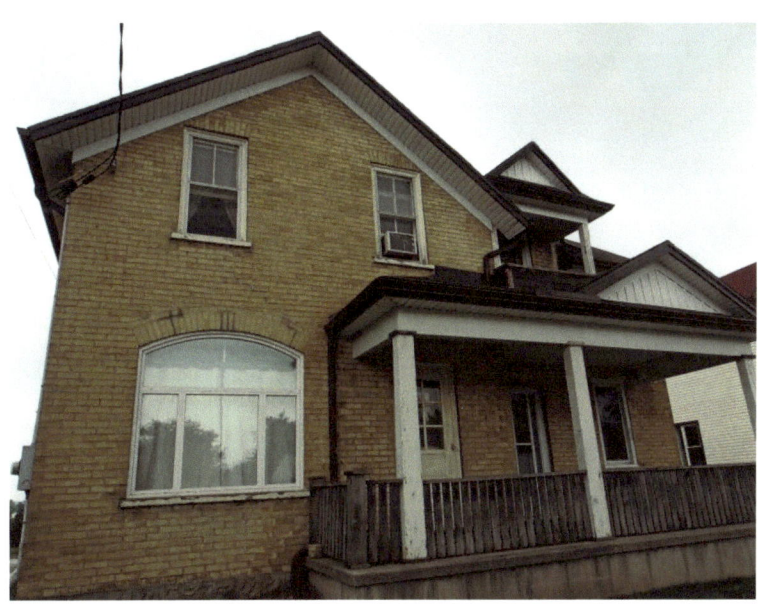

Lobsinger Line – Gothic Revival

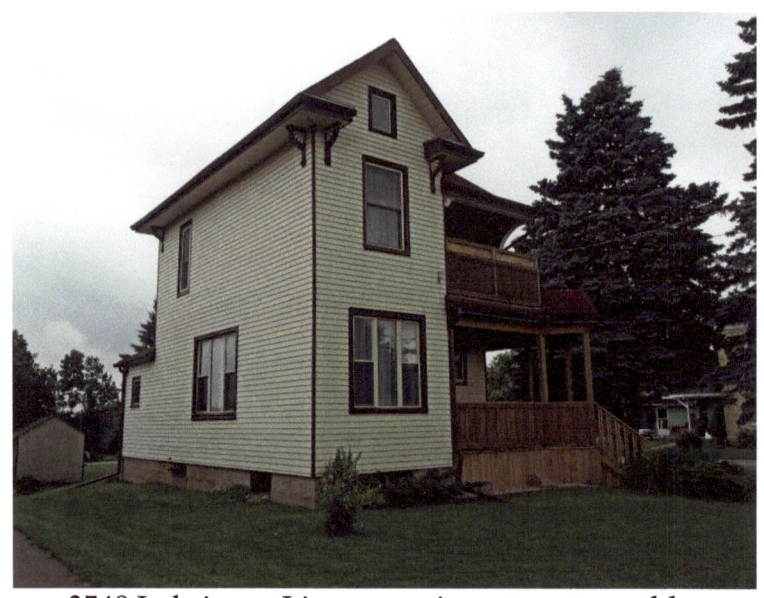

3540 Lobsinger Line – cornice return on gable, cornice brackets

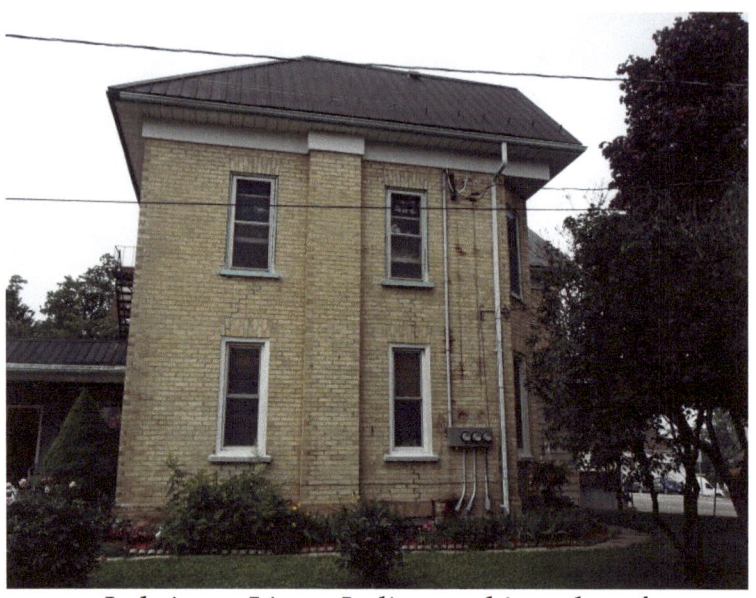

Lobsinger Line – Italianate, hipped roof

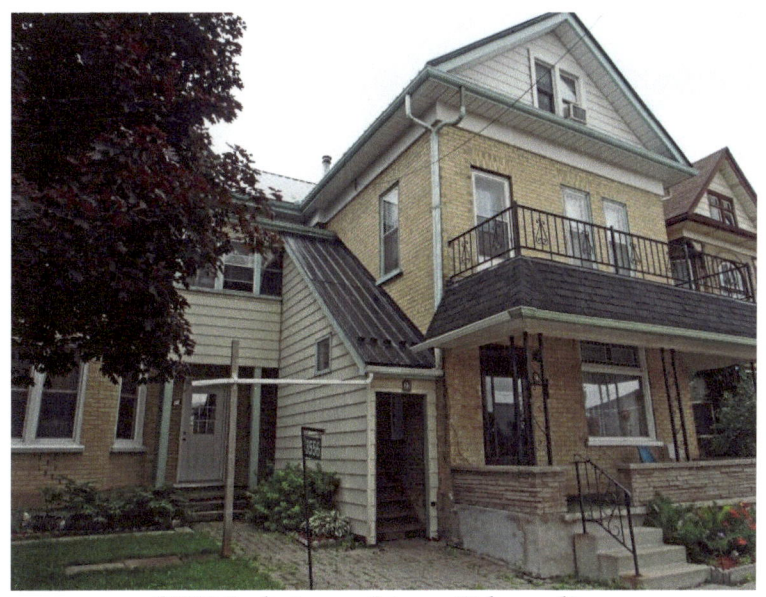

3556 Lobsinger Line - Edwardian

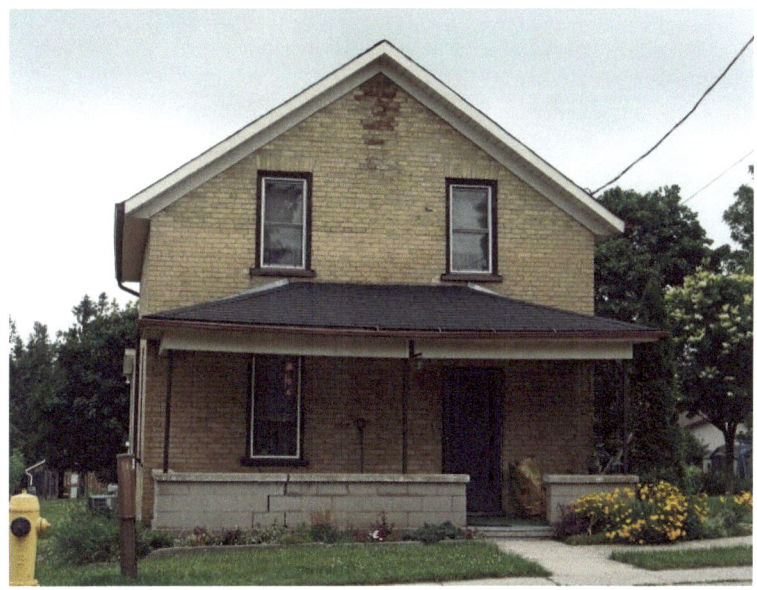

3551 Lobsinger Line – Gothic Revival

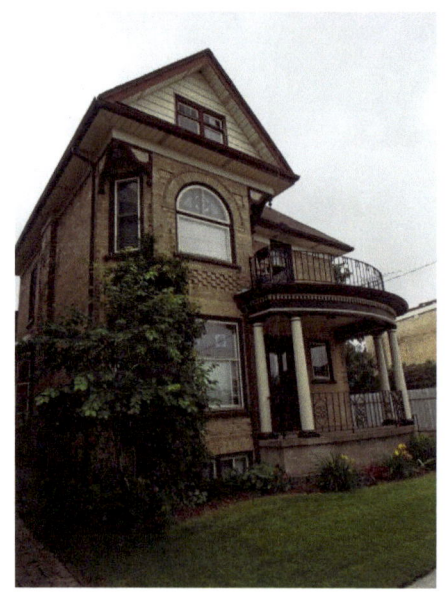

3560 Lobsinger Line - Edwardian

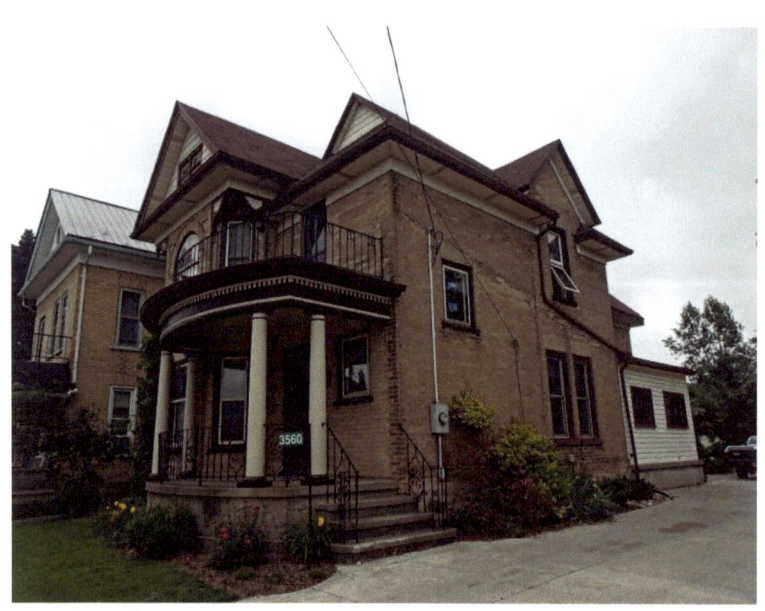

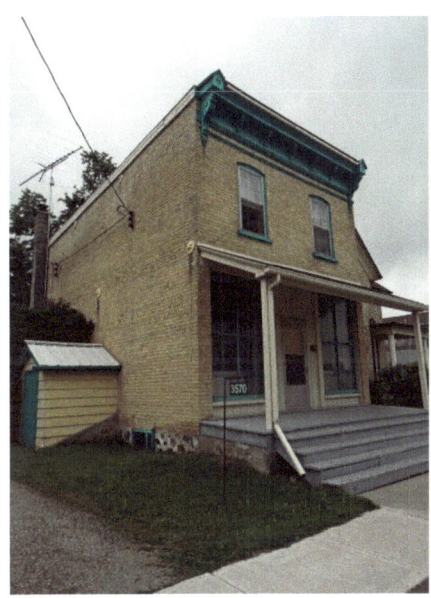

3570 Lobsinger Line
Italianate

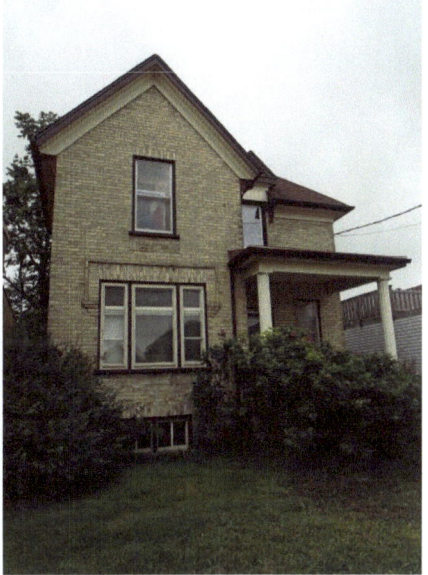

3580 Lobsinger Line
Gothic Revival

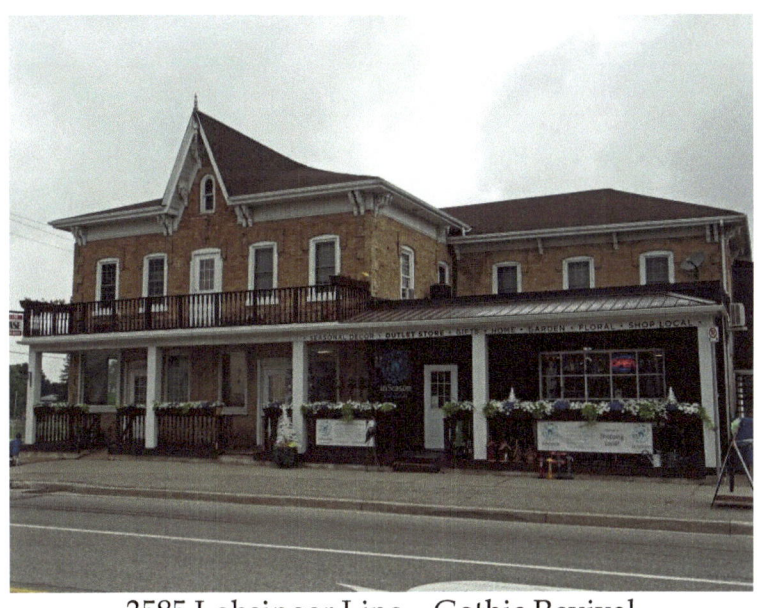

3585 Lobsinger Line – Gothic Revival

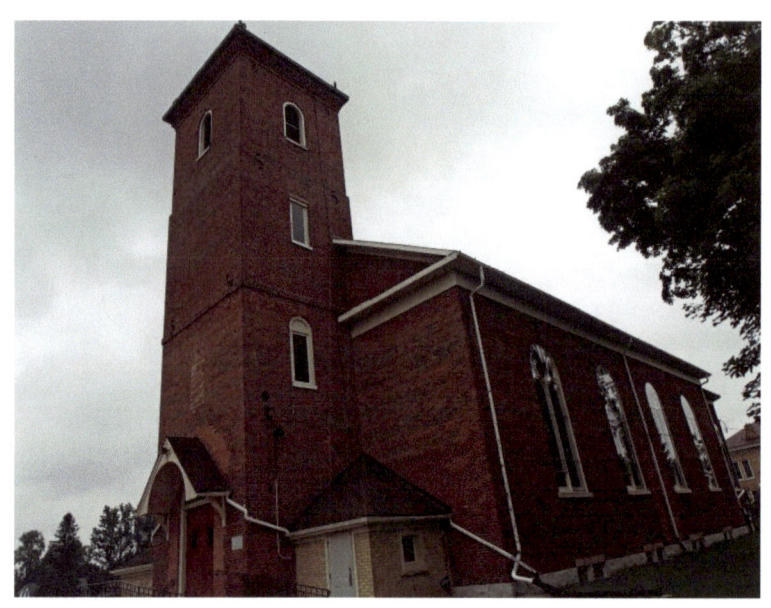

Saint Clements Roman Catholic Church c. 1858
3629 Lobsinger Line

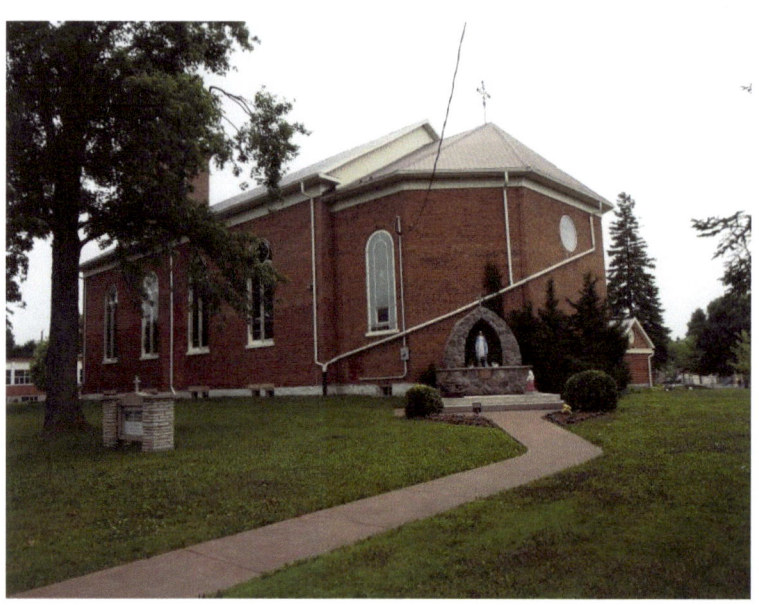

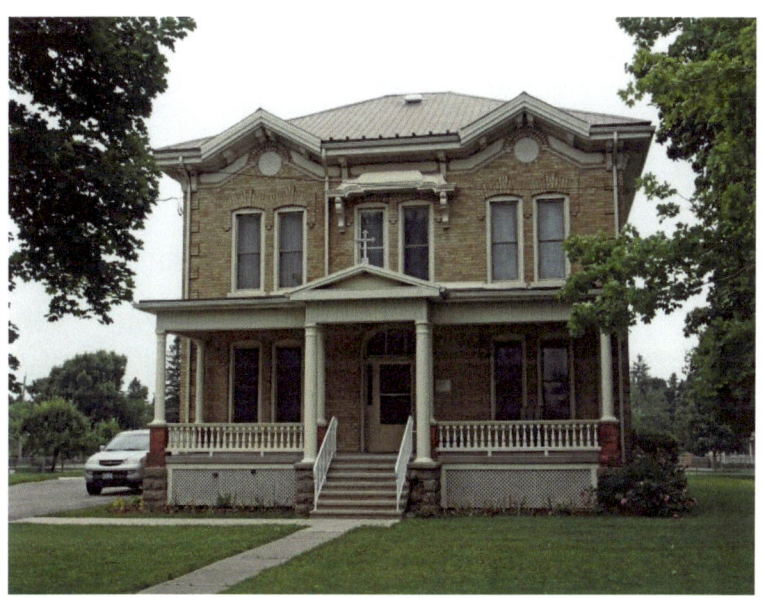

Lobsinger Line – Italianate, hipped roof, pediment

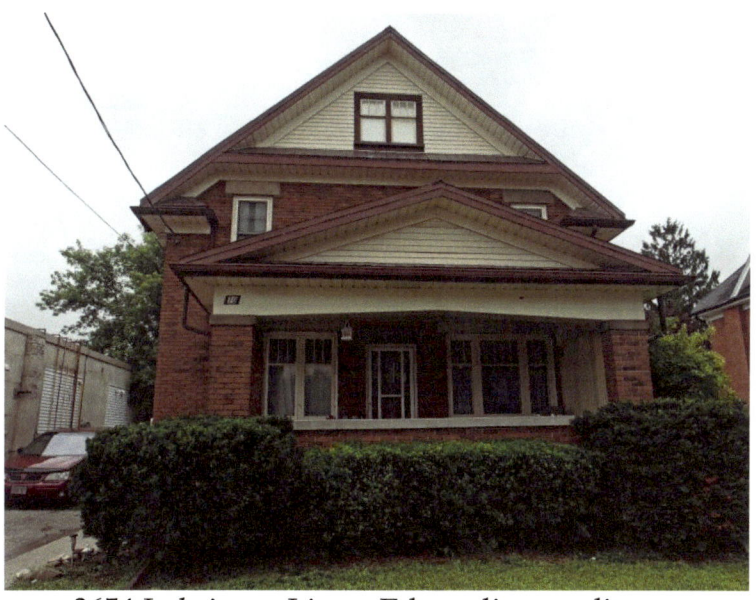

3654 Lobsinger Line – Edwardian, pediment

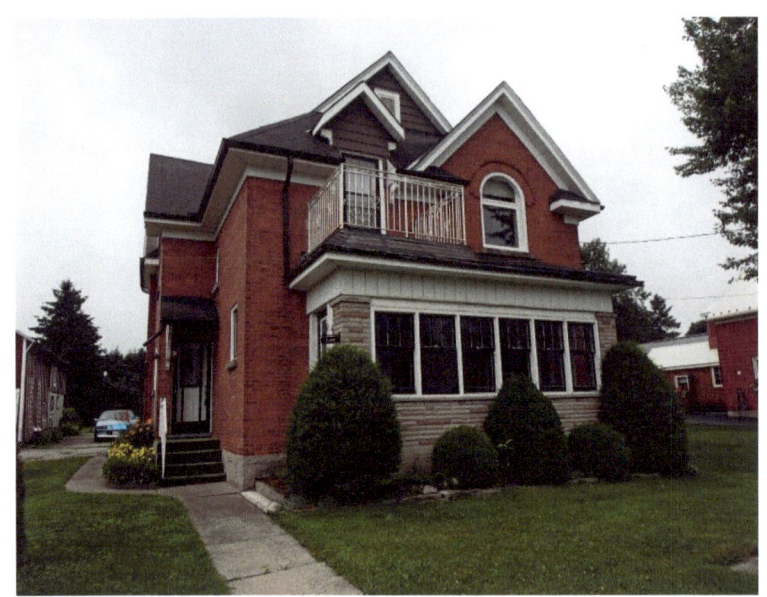

3658 Lobsinger Line

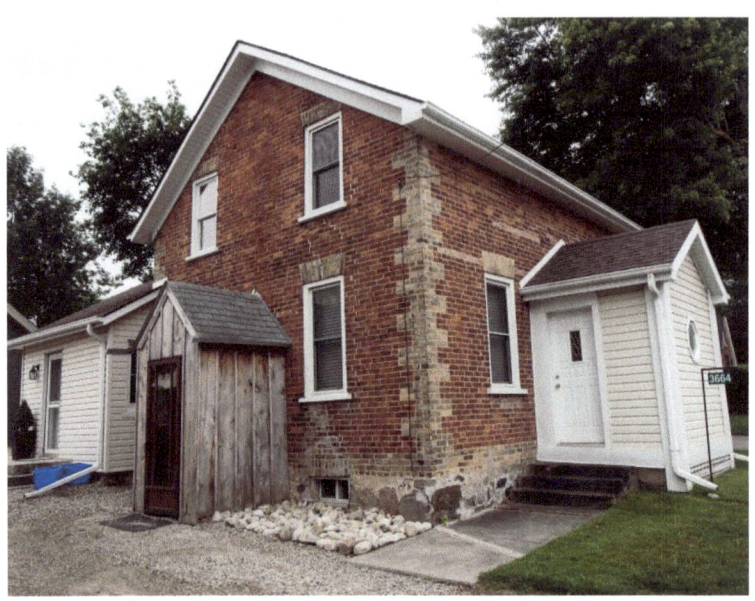

3664 Lobsinger Line – Gothic Revival, corner quoins

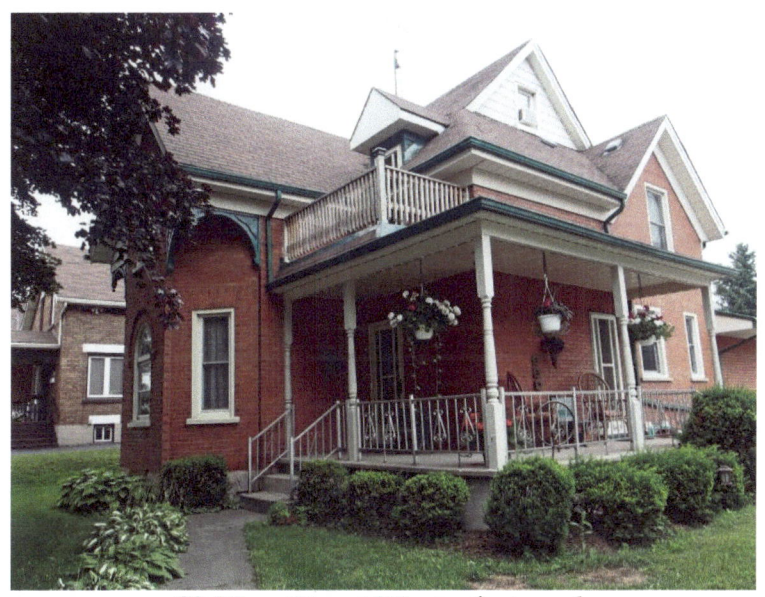

83 King Street West - fretwork

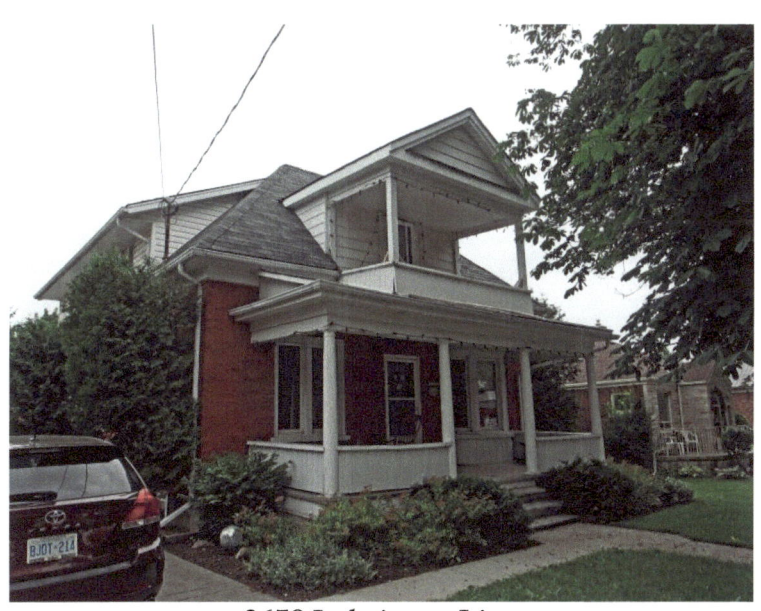

3659 Lobsinger Line

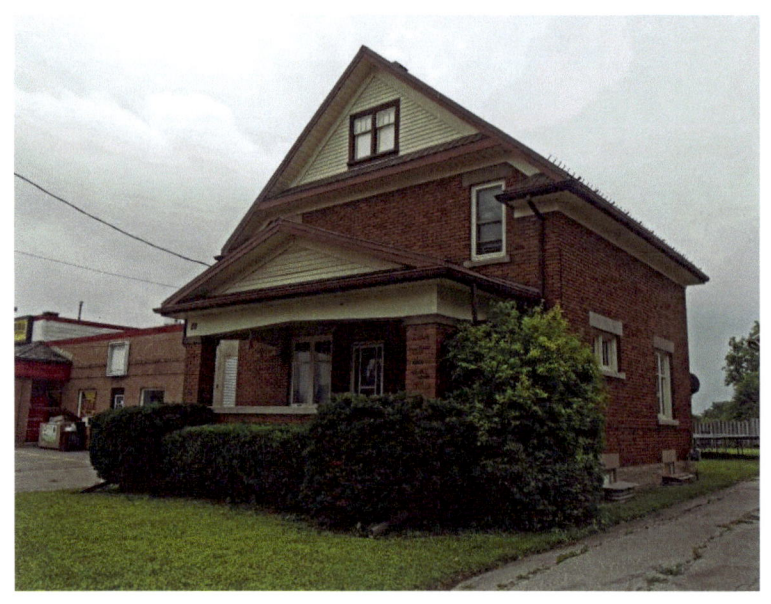

Lobsinger Line

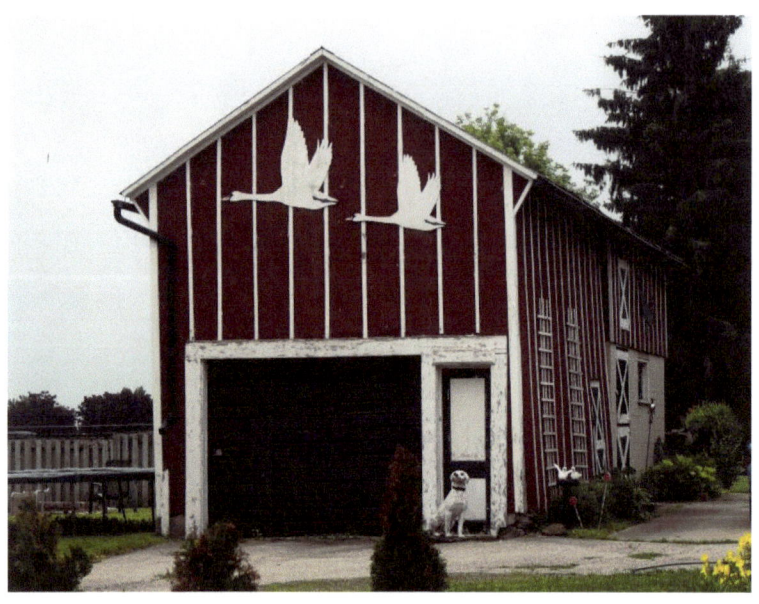

Heidelberg

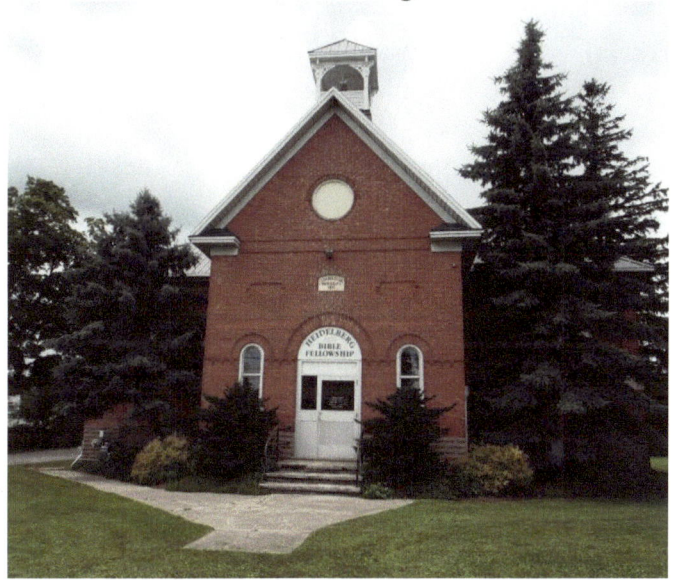

Heidelberg School Union Section 11 c 1911
now Heidelberg Bible Fellowship

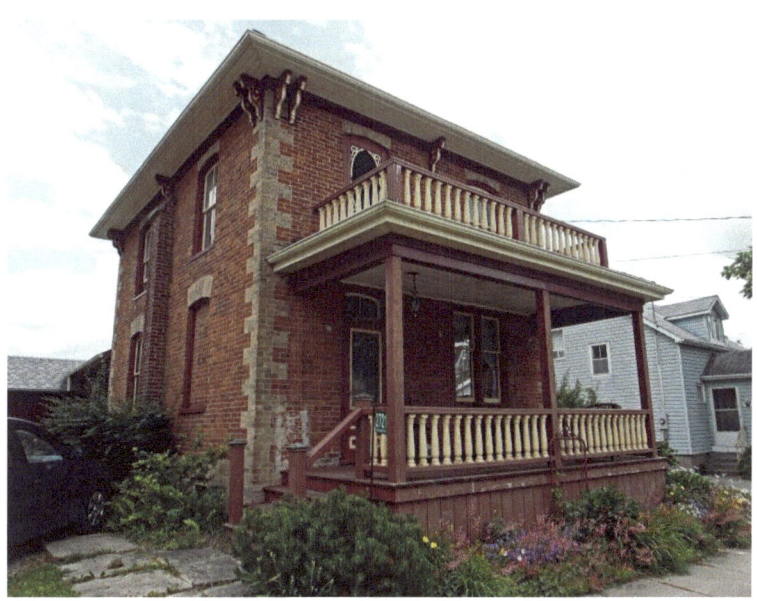

2735 Kressler Road – Italianate, cornice brackets,
corner quoins

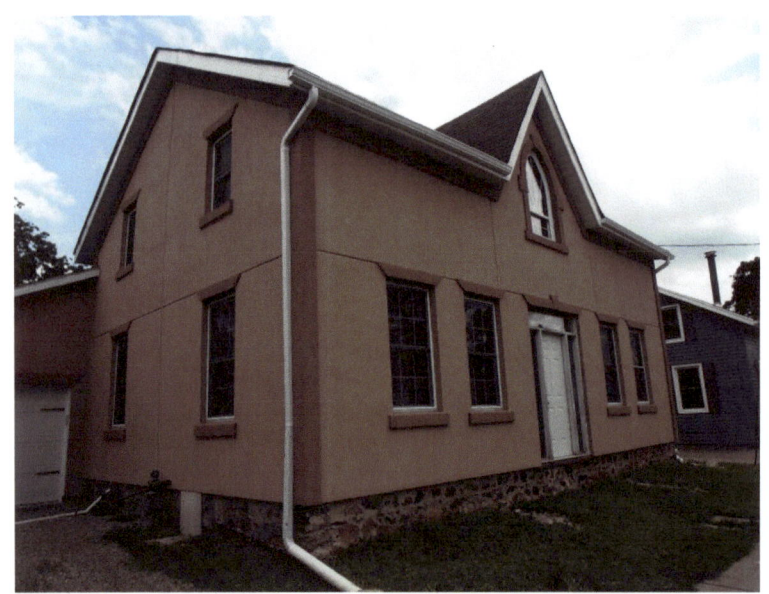

2735 Kressler Road – Gothic Revival

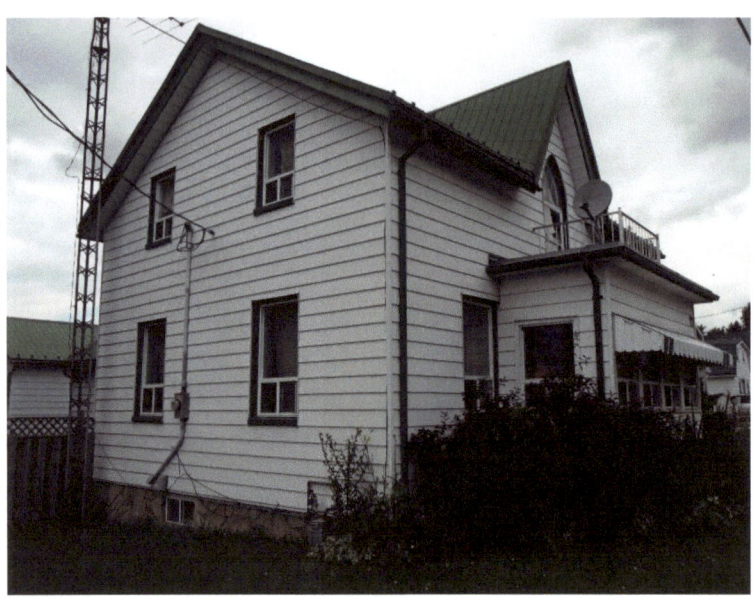

"12" Kressler Road – Gothic Revival

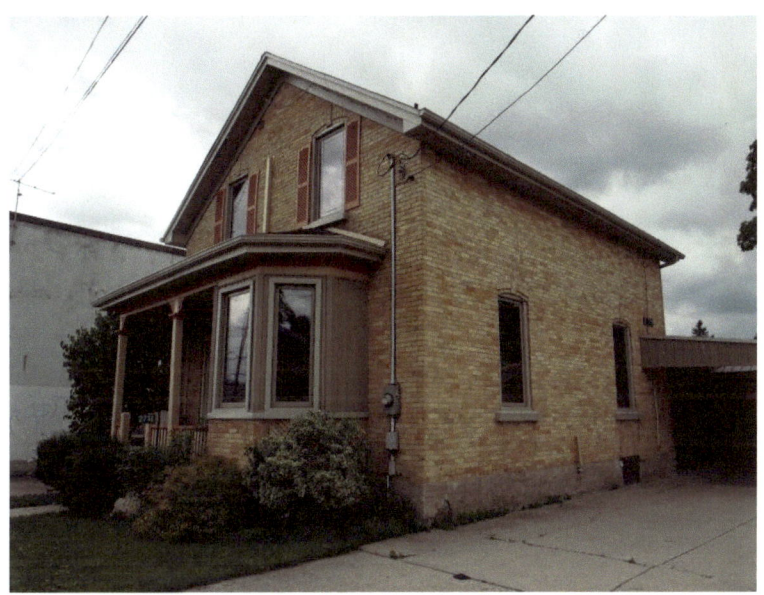

2714 Kressler Road – Gothic Revival

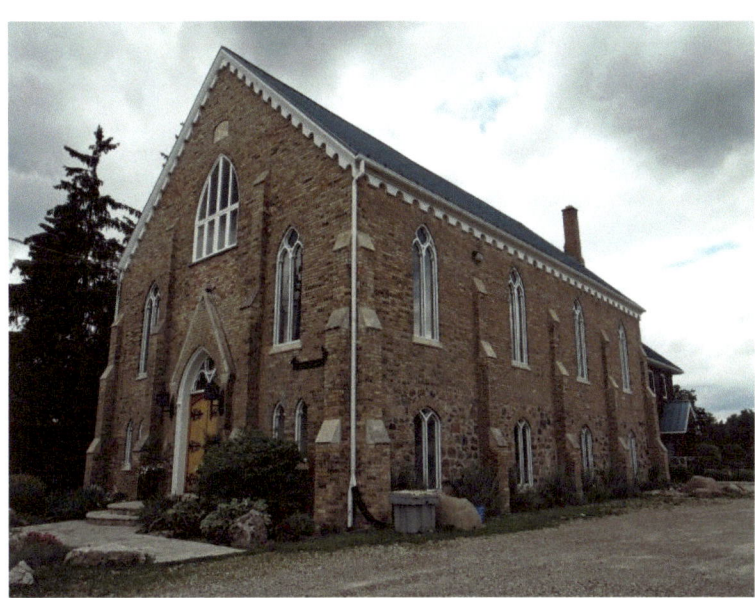

2965 Lobsinger Line former church c 1872 now Hauser Hall
Cobblestone on lower wall, lancet windows

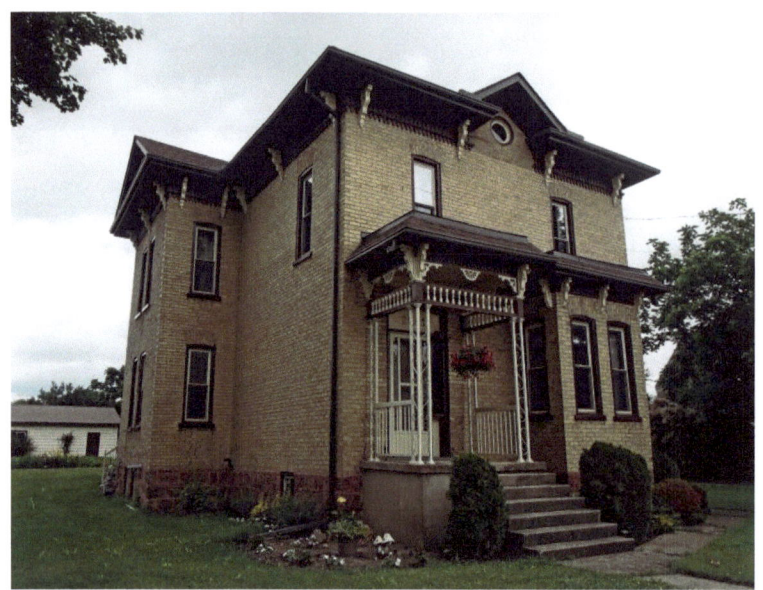

2941 Lobsinger Line – Italianate, cornice brackets

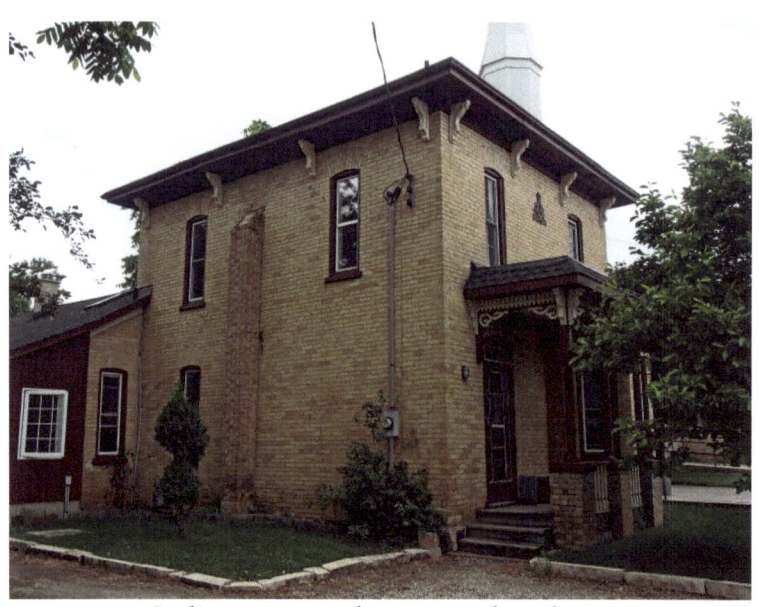

Italianate, single cornice brackets

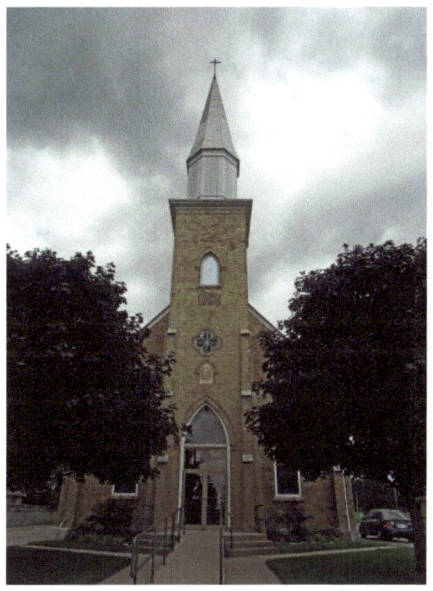

2925 Lobsinger Line – St. Peters Evangelical Lutheran Church
c. 1869

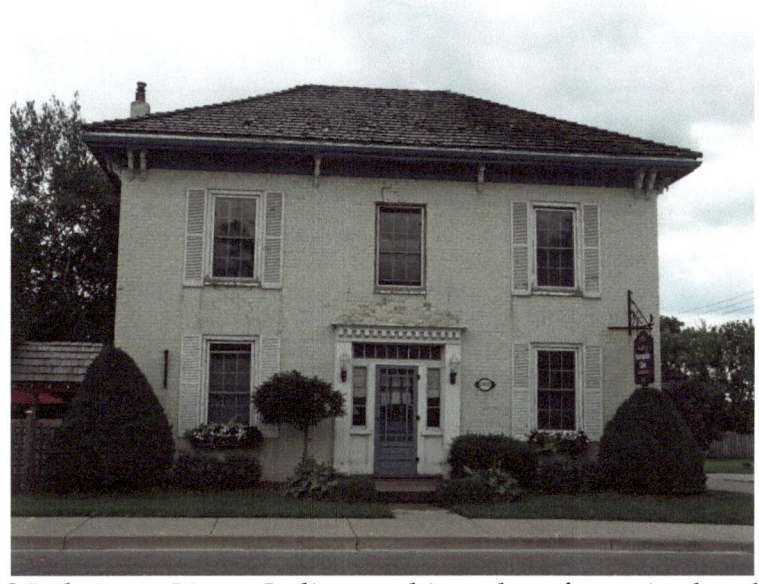

2932 Lobsinger Line – Italianate, hipped roof, cornice brackets

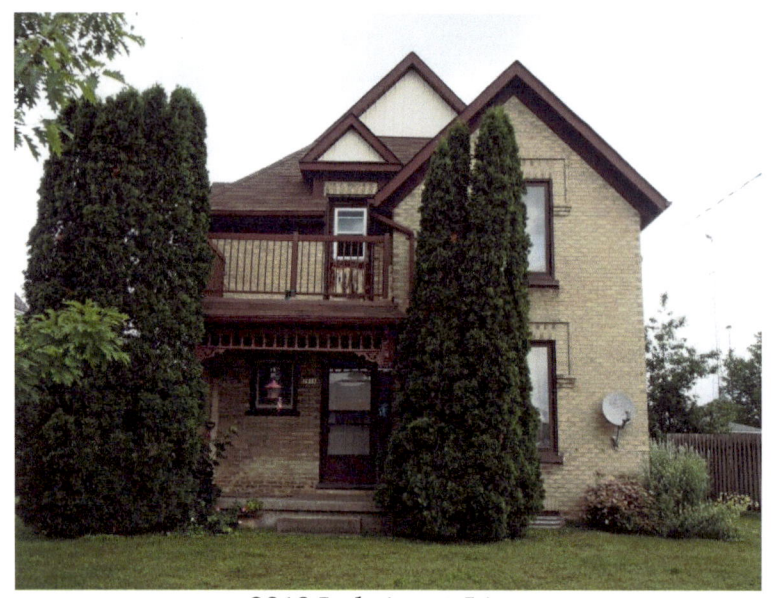

2919 Lobsinger Line

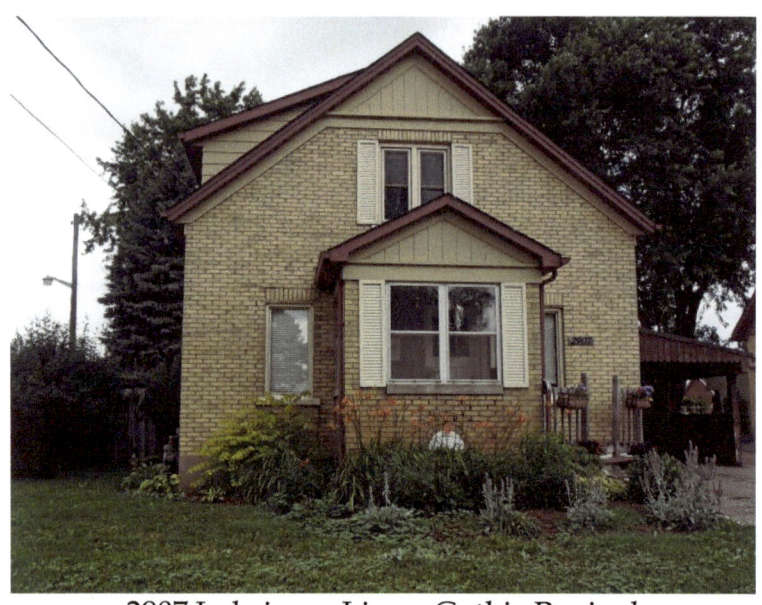

2907 Lobsinger Line – Gothic Revival

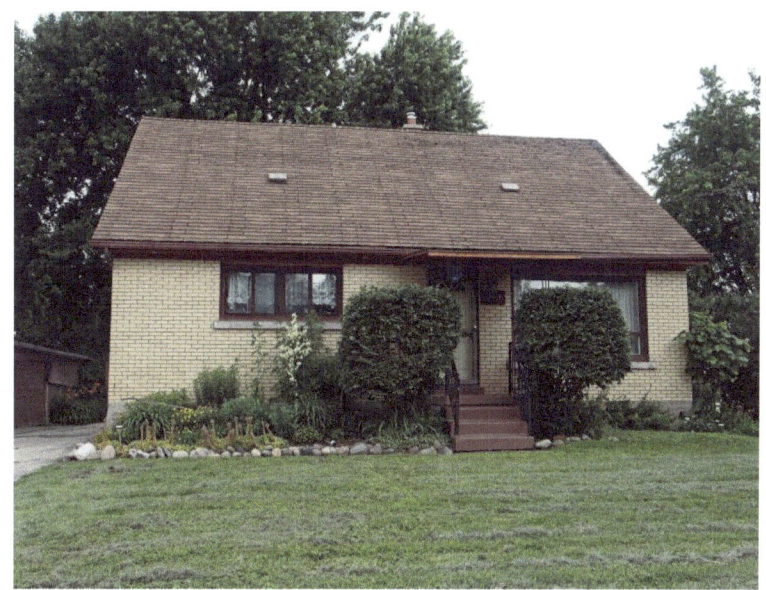

2901 Lobsinger Line

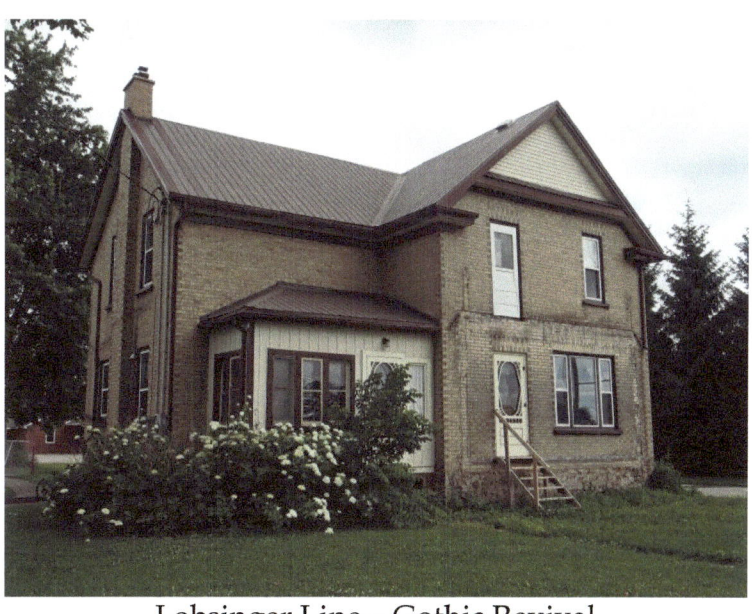

Lobsinger Line – Gothic Revival

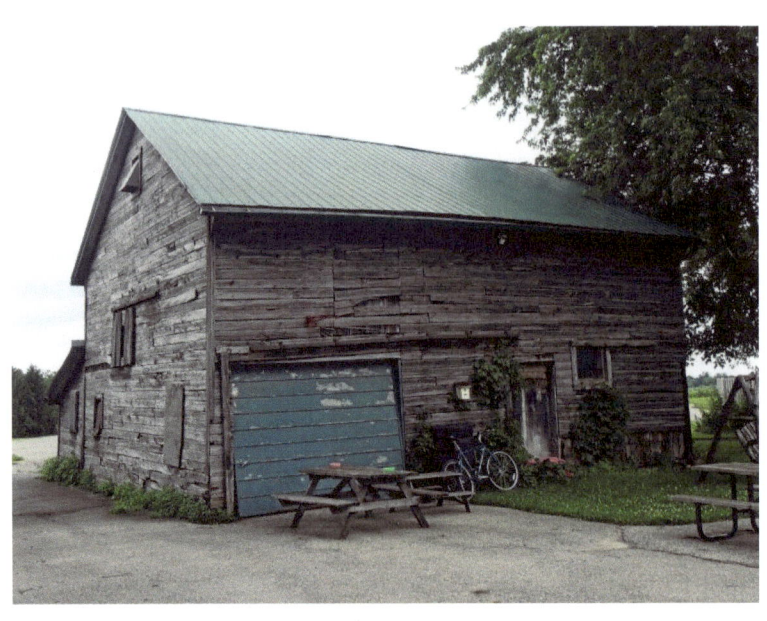

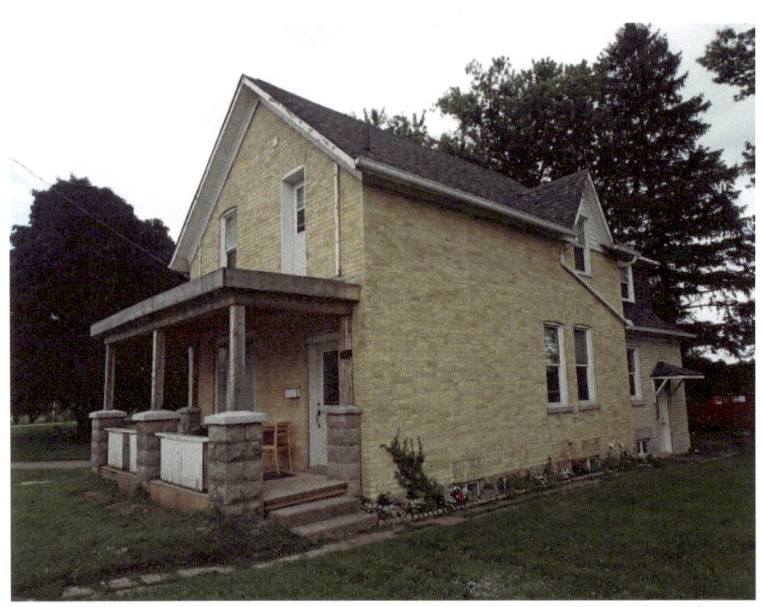

Lobsinger Line – Gothic Revival in yellow brick

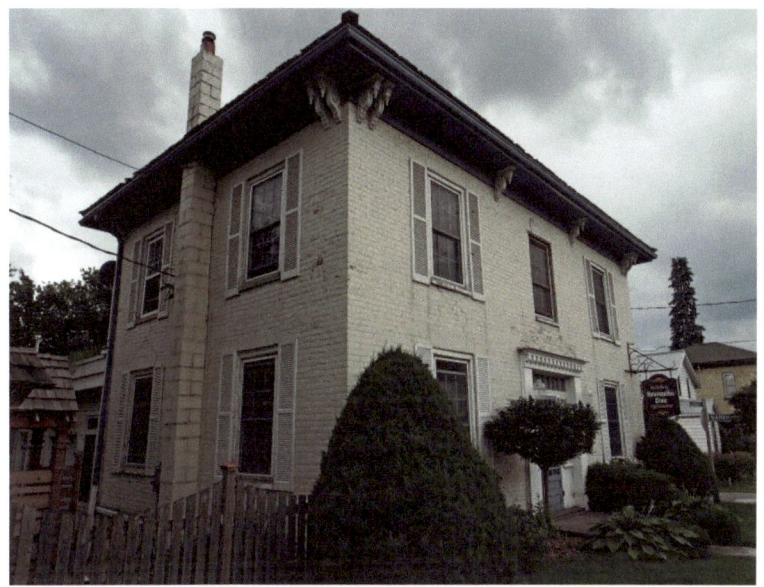

2931 Lobsinger Line – Italianate, cornice brackets

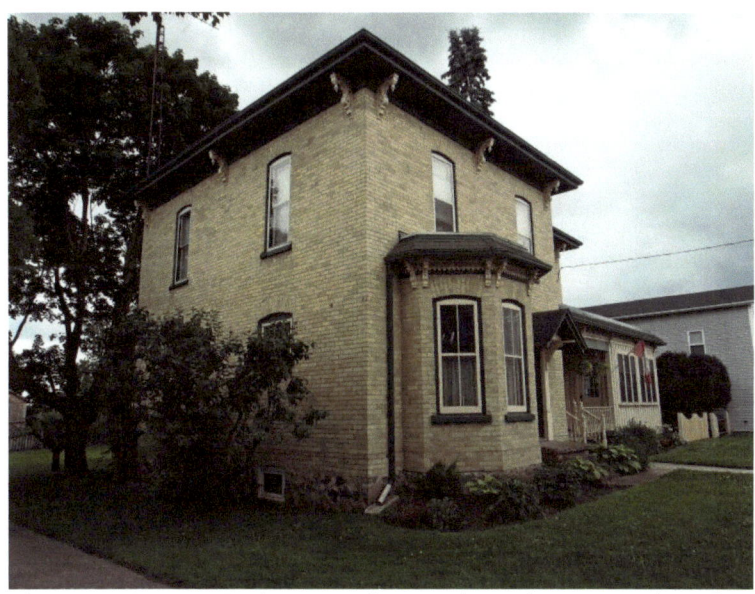

Lobsinger Line – Italianate, hipped roof, cornice brackets,
bay window on ground floor

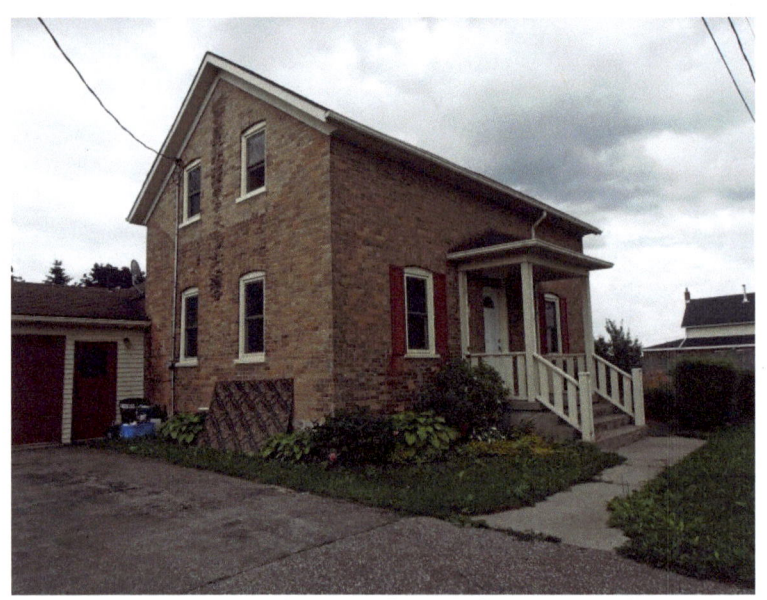

2685 Kressler Road – Gothic Revival

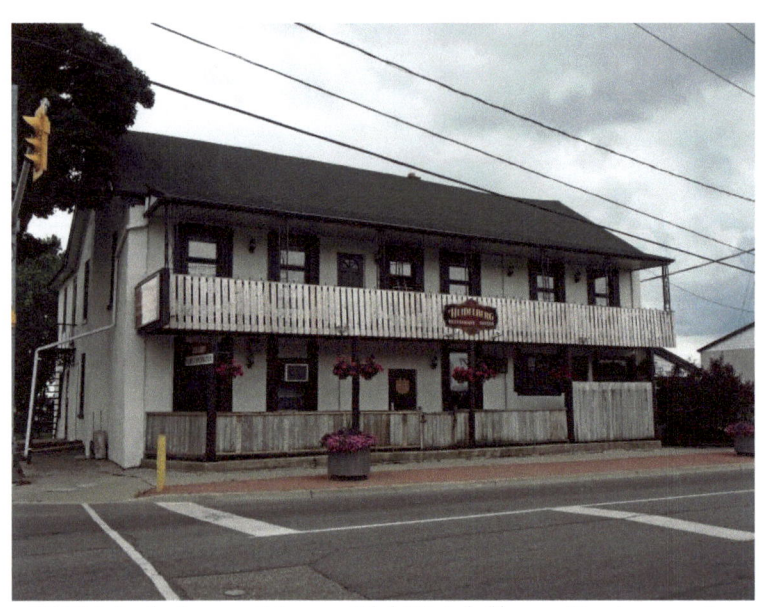

3006 Lobsinger Line - Old Heidelberg Restaurant,
Tavern and Motel – Georgian style

Crosshill

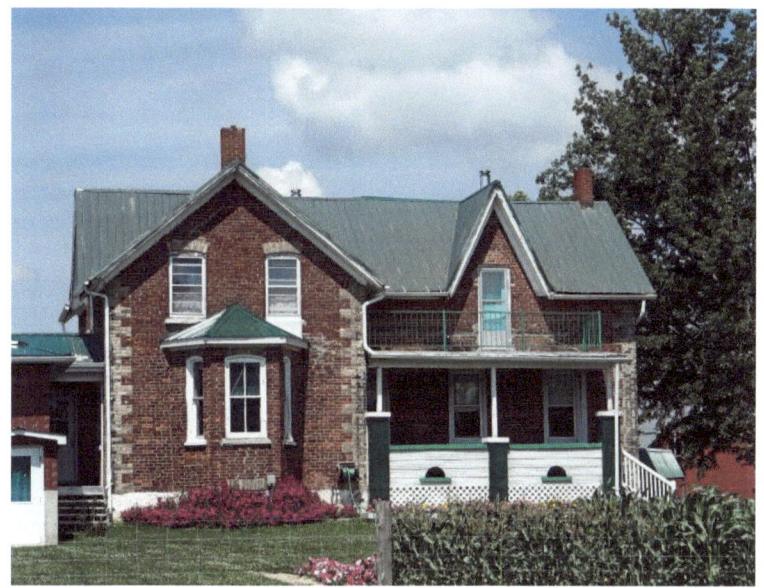

Gothic Revival, corner quoins

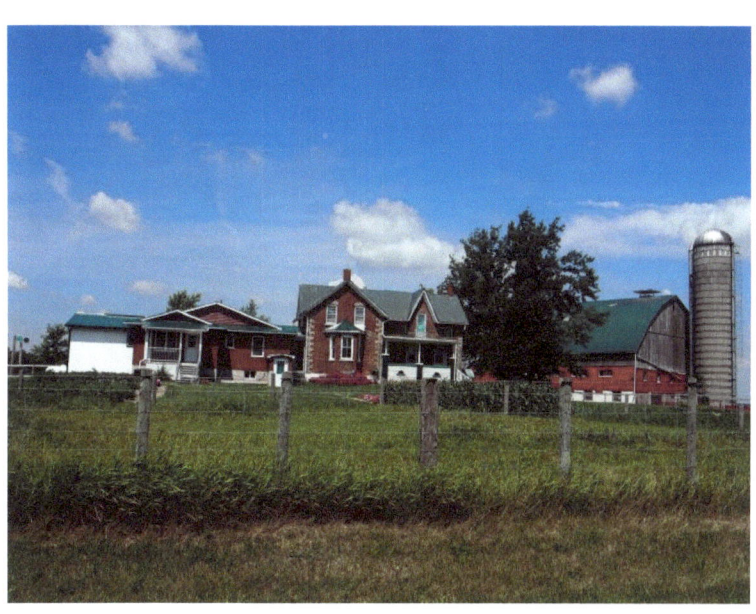

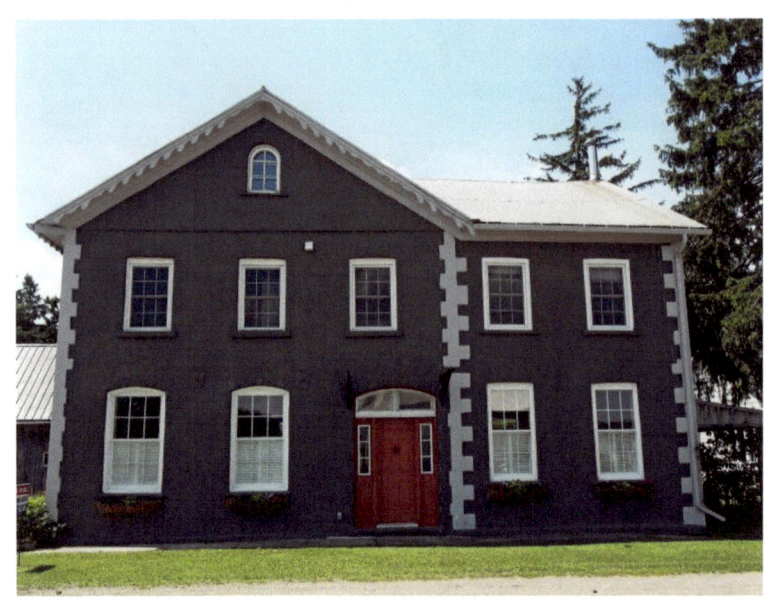

#4830 – original red brick plastered over and painted grey

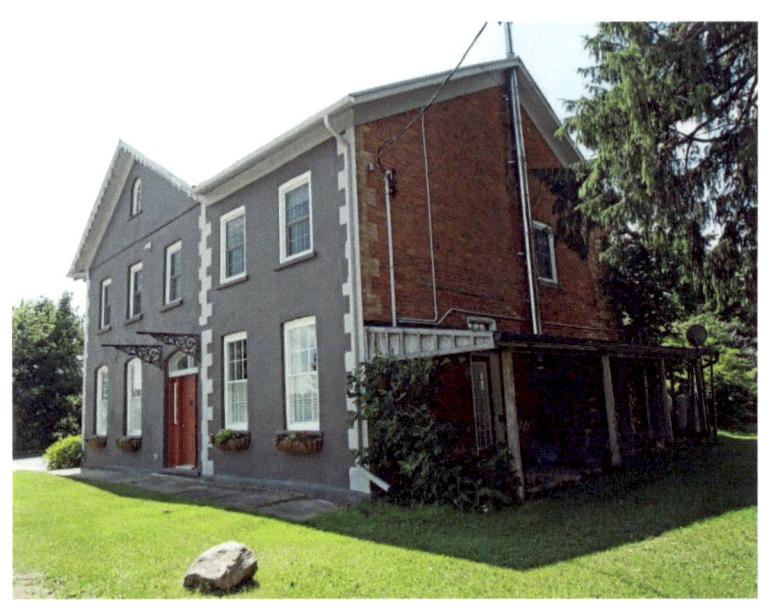

Corner quoins

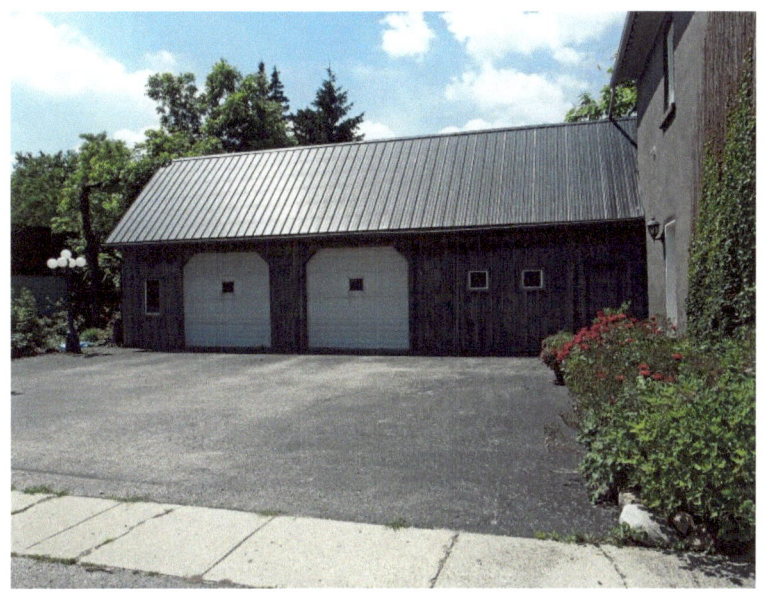

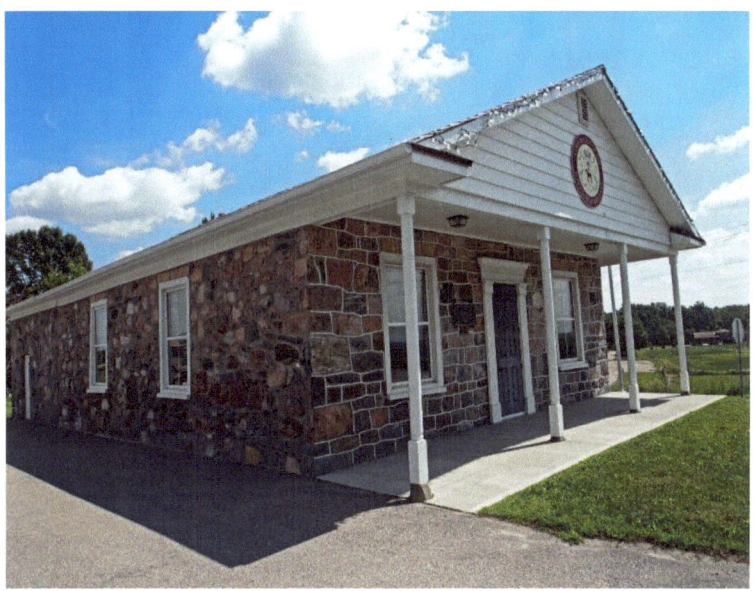

#4805 - Wellesley Township Hall Crosshill – 1855
– chosen because of its central location - cobblestone

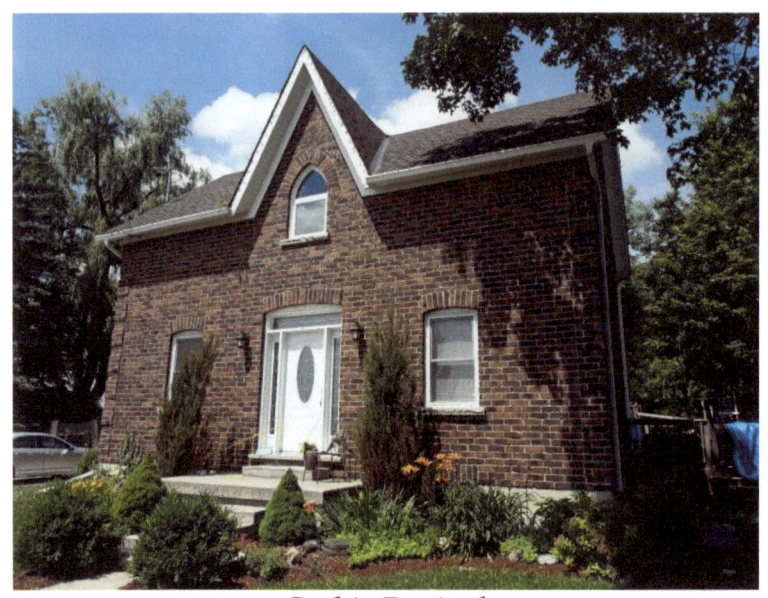

Gothic Revival

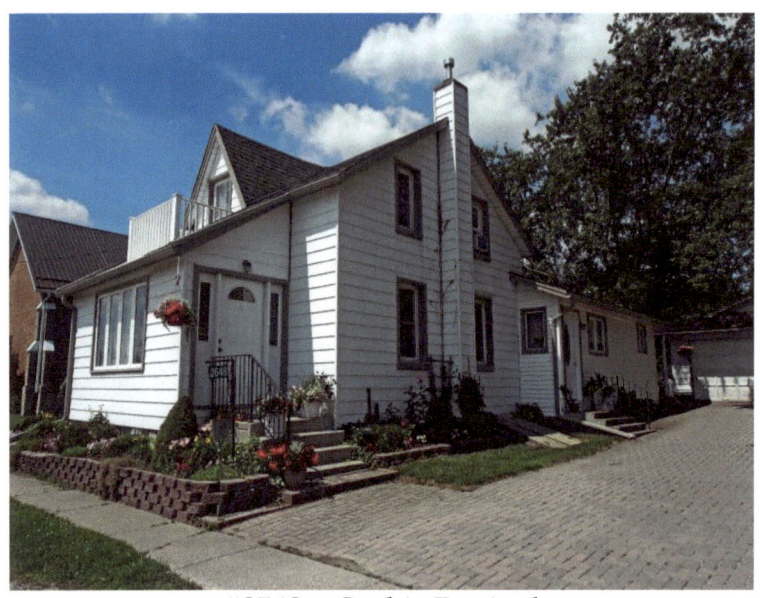

#2548 – Gothic Revival

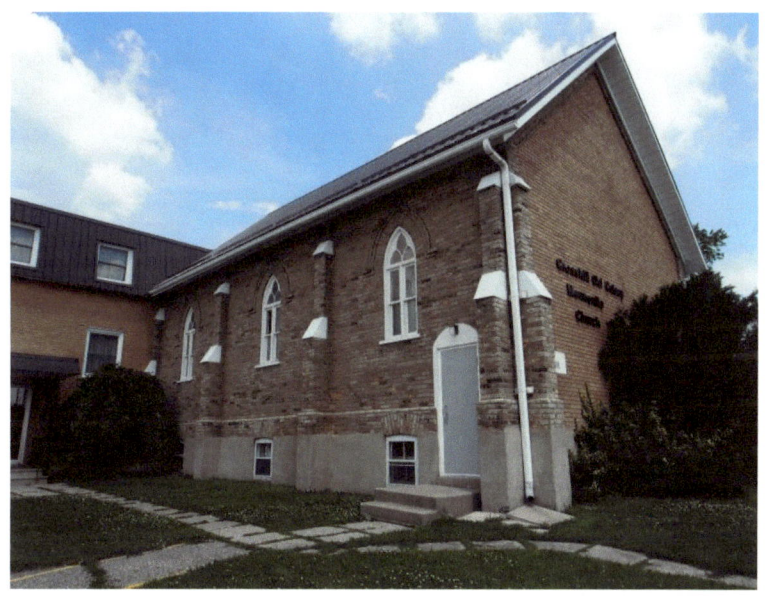

#2640 – Crosshill Old Colony Mennonite Church c. 1888

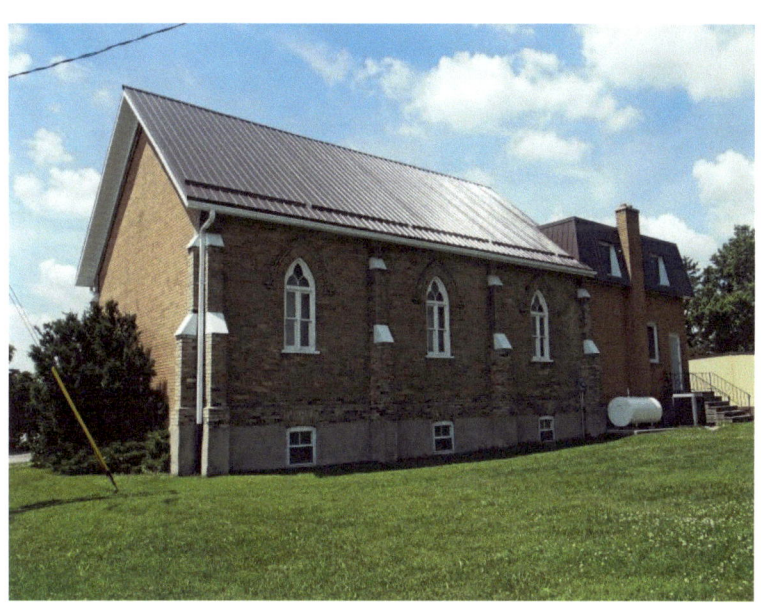

Bamberg

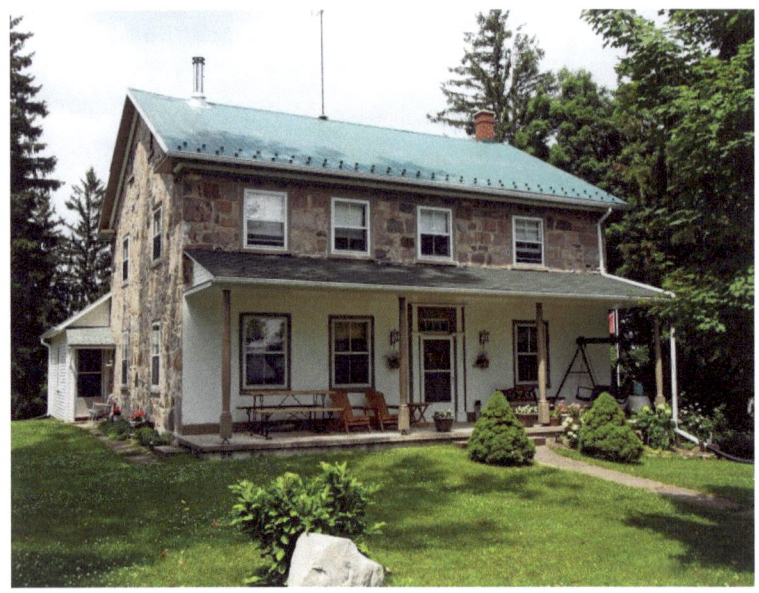

Cobblestone house and shed

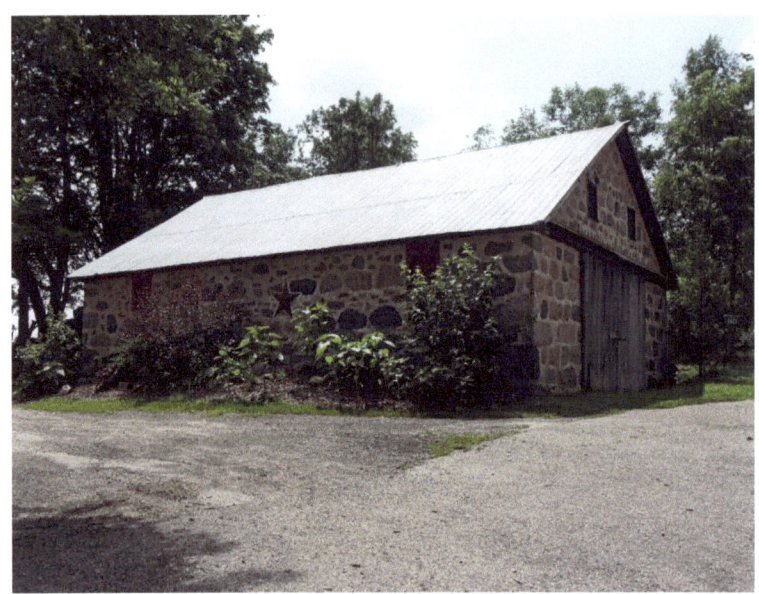

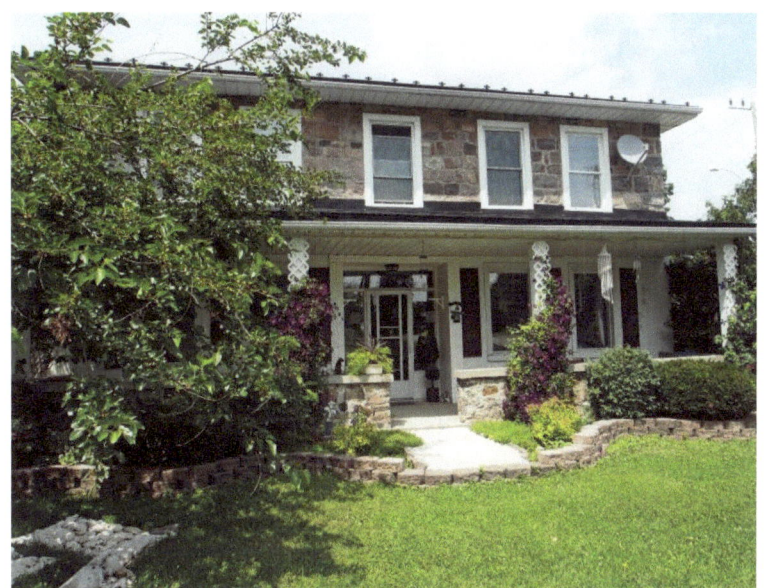

4107 Moser-Young Drive - cobblestone

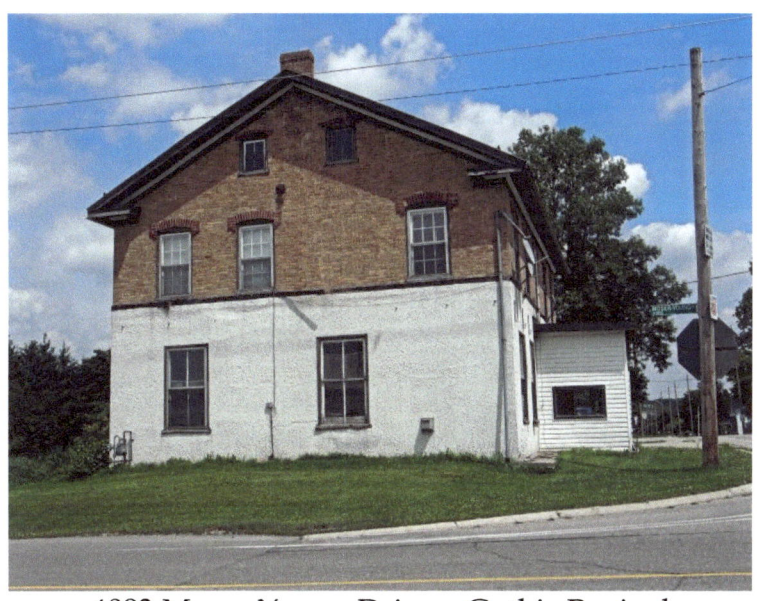

4093 Moser-Young Drive – Gothic Revival

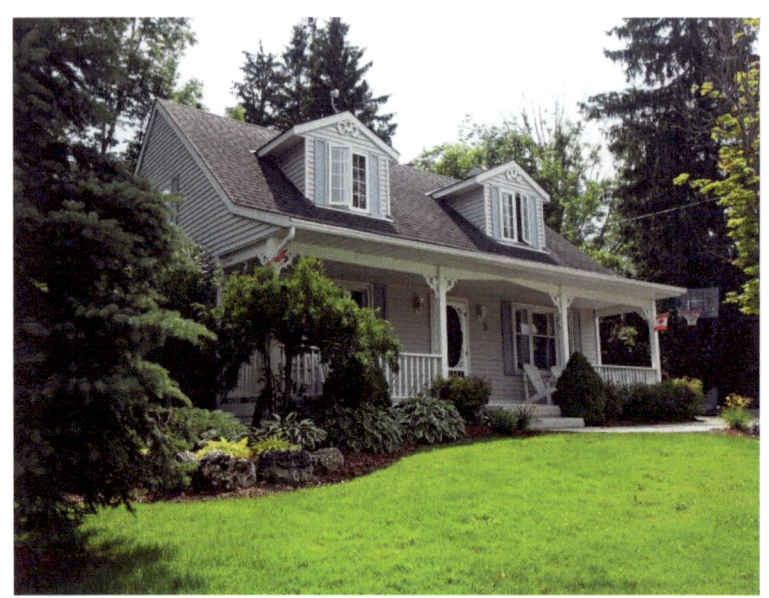

Weimar Line – dormers in attic

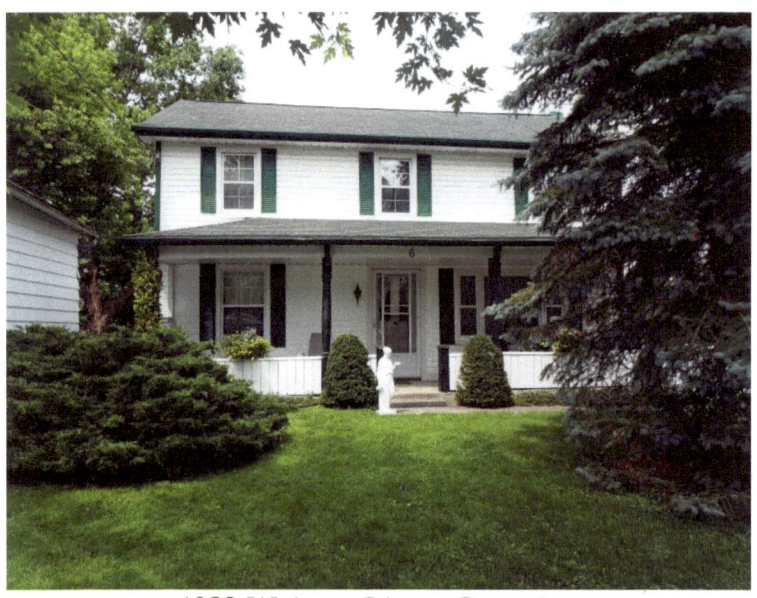

4083 Weimar Line - Georgian

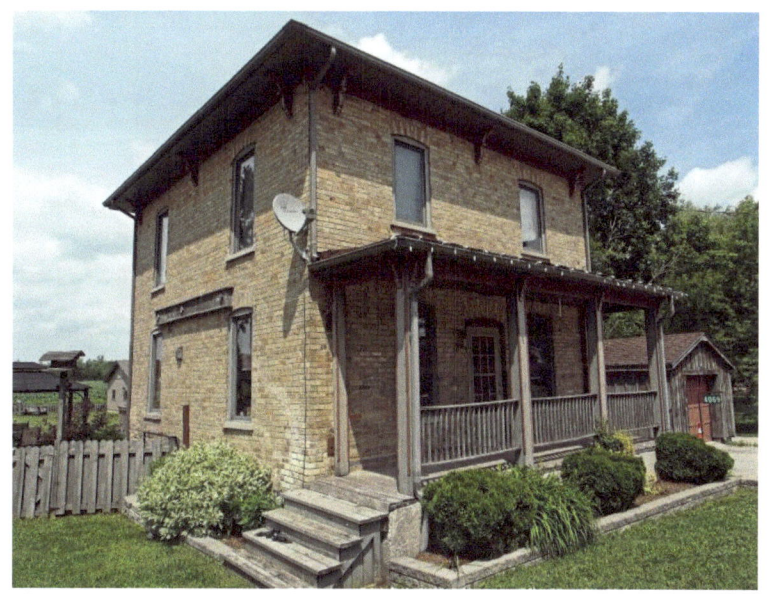

4069 Weimar Line – Italianate, hipped roof, cornice brackets

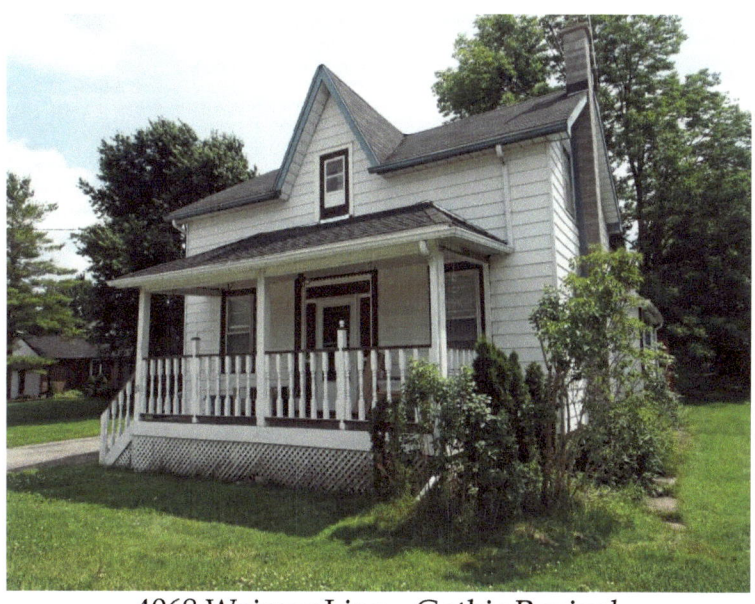

4068 Weimar Line – Gothic Revival

Brackets: a decorative or weight-bearing structural element which forms a right angle with one side against a wall and the other under a projecting surface such as an eave or roof. Example: Lobsinger Line, Heidelberg	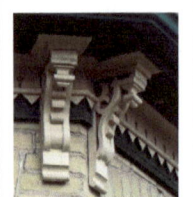
Cobblestone architecture: Refers to the use of cobblestones embedded in mortar as a method for erecting walls on houses and commercial buildings. Example: 40 Young Street, St. Jacobs	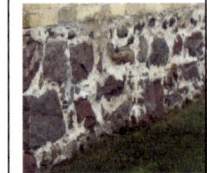
Cornice: originally the wooden overhang of the roof. With the use of stone, brick, iron and steel, the cornice is any projecting shelf at the top of a ceiling or roof. They can be very decorative. Example: 36 Young Street, St. Jacobs	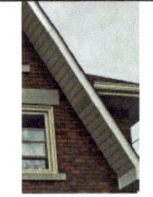
Cornice Return: decorative element on the end of a gable. Example: 3465 Lobsinger Line, St. Clements	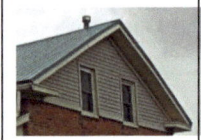
Dentil Moulding: an even series of rectangles used as ornamental decoration in cornices. Example: The Old Factory, Cedar Street, St. Jacobs	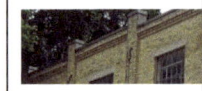

Dormer: (French for "sleep") a gable end window that pierces through the plane of a sloping roof surface to create usable space in the top floor or attic of a building by adding headroom. Example: Weimar Line, Bamberg	
Gable: the triangular portion of a wall between the edges of a sloping roof. Example: Darryl Sittler house, St. Jacobs	
Hipped Roof: a roof where all sides slope downwards to the walls with no gables. Example: Lobsinger Line, St. Clements	
Lancet Window: a tall, narrow window with a pointed arch at its top. Example: 2965 Lobsinger Line former church, now Hauser Hall, Heidelberg	
Pediment: a triangular section above the horizontal structure (entablature), typically supported by columns. The inside of the triangle is called the tympanum. Example: Lobsinger Line, St. Clements	

Quoin: masonry blocks at the corner of a wall, often a decorative feature, usually larger or of a different colour than the rest of the wall. Example: 3664 Lobsinger Line, St. Clements	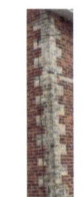
Rose Window: a circular window with ornamental tracery radiating from the centre. Example: 2925 Lobsinger Line, St. Peter's Evangelical Lutheran Church, Heidelberg	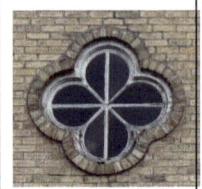
Vergeboard and Finial: also called bargeboards – hang from the projecting end of a roof and are often elaborately carved and ornamented. **Finial:** ornament added to the top of a gable, pinnacle, canopy or spire – a Gothic element. Example: 7 Cedar Street East, St. Jacobs	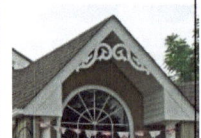

Building Styles

Edwardian, 1900-1930 – This style bridges the ornate and elaborate styles of the Victorian era and the simplified styles of the 20th century. Balanced facades, simple roof lines, dormer windows, large front porches, and smooth brick surfaces are its characteristics. Example: 17 Young Street, St. Jacobs	
Georgian, before 1860 – This style began with the British King Georges in the 18th century. These buildings have balanced facades around a central door, medium-pitched gable roofs, and small paned windows. Example: 3006 Lobsinger Line - Old Heidelberg Restaurant, Tavern and Motel	
Gothic Revival, 1830-1890 – These decorative buildings have sharply-pitched gables with highly detailed vergeboards, pointed-arch window openings, and dichromatic brickwork. It is a common style in Ontario. Example: 35 Young Street, St. Jacobs	
Italianate, 1850-1900 – It has wide-bracketed eaves, belvederes, wrap-around verandahs. Example: Lobsinger Line, St. Clements	
Queen Anne, 1885-1900 – This style is distinguished by an irregular outline featuring a combination of an offset tower, broad gables, projecting two-storey bays, verandahs, multi-sloped roofs, and tall, decorative chimneys. A mixture of brick and wood is common. Windows often have one large single-paned bottom sash and small panes in the upper sash. Example: 29 Albert Street, St. Jacobs	

www.ingramcontent.com/pod-product-compliance
Lightning Source LLC
Chambersburg PA
CBHW040848180526
45159CB00001B/354